Gender Incongruent: Understanding Us

Tracy C. Coyle

For my family

TABLE OF CONTENTS

PREFACE

This has been a difficult book to write. So many emotions and memories touched upon that there were times when even a single paragraph took hours to write. And then I had to compare them to what others have said to me over the years, and many are repeating even today.

We are not the result of some grooming, or sexualization, or ideological corruption. We are not engaging in some fetish desires. The vast majority of us just want to have normal lives. But neither side in the political arguments is actually interested in discussing real issues. I argue almost daily against the trans activist's efforts in the trans community that promote false statements and unrealistic hopes. I argue almost daily against the efforts to ban trans health care, and even the arguments against our actual existence, though if you get the actual person to listen, they often will acknowledge there 'are a few' that might really need the help.

There are references to studies and journal articles. You will be able to find others that come to the complete opposite conclusions. Such is the state of science in this area. The science is not settled. Which leaves room for ideologues on both sides.

I am trying to stay focused on what gender incongruent people face. Yet, it is so hard not to point out the extreme disconnect between the individual gender incongruent person and the political demands ostensibly being made on their behalf.

It is an attempt to help you understand us, outside of the political posturing from both sides.

INTRODUCTION

What do we mean by gender incongruent? When does this 'incongruity' develop? How does it start? How does someone know they are incongruent? You might have these and lots of other questions, but we generally only have two related ones: Why did this happen to me? Why can't I be normal?

*

At the cellular level, chromosomes dictate how we are to be, but that involves millions of individual processes during natal development. They determine everything from minor attributes like the color of our hair, to the major functions like reproductive organs. Chromosomes define our biological sex, male or female[1]. They are with us for our entire existence, and they remain unchanged throughout. So, if you have chromosomes that code for male or female when you are born, you will still have them when you die. Nothing we can do at this point in time changes that.

Our physical sex consists of the reproductive organs and genitalia with which you are born. Of course, it also relates to a large base of physical attributes affected by puberty such as skeletal and muscular structures. This is what people see when they look at you. However, people see what you present to them. Depending on your appearance, clothing, mannerisms, and other factors, people could see something very different than the physical reality. People who are androgynous, whose appearance is inconsistent or diverges from the expected, can confuse onlookers. Usually, it is not the intent of the person to confuse, but their appearance being outside the expected norms leads that way.

Gender identity is the psychological foundation that supports your awareness of both your biological and physical sex. It is biologically based, but also something that takes time for you to become aware of. It takes

---

[1] X and Y chromosomal aneuploidies (the presence of an abnormal number of sex chromosome) are among the most common human whole-chromosomal copy number variations, with an estimated incidence in the general population between 1 in 400 to 1 in 1,000 [1,2–4] for each of the sex Chromosome syndromes: Department of Pediatrics, George Washington University School of Medicine and Health Sciences https://journals.plos.org/plosone/article?id=10.1371/journal.pone.0161045

time for your 'self' identity to be recognized and as it does, details are added, including the awareness of biological sex. Those whose gender identity is consistent with their biological/physical sex are called congruent (or cisgender). This happens more than 99% of the time!

If you cannot accept that this happens, regardless of the frequency, then the rest of this book is not for you. If you can at least be agnostic about it, read on.

*

We have been dealing with our gender incongruity all our lives, from our earliest memories. We didn't wake up one morning and just decided to be, something different.

For decades people explained that we were 'a man trapped in a woman's body' or 'a woman trapped in a man's body.' This phrase haunts us. It takes a complex issue and presents it as an emotionally driven phenomenon easily dismissed by 'realists'. While many other formulations get used, we learn that our brain has developed according to the biological norms of one sex, while our body has developed according to the physical attributes of the other.

The how and why of gender incongruity is still a matter of research. What is clear is that for a small subset of the human population, somewhere between .25 and .4 percent[2,3], the congruity between gender identity and chromosomal/physical foundations fails to form in natal development. The current prevalence is estimated at **1 in 2,800** for incongruent males and **1 in 5,200** for incongruent females.[4]

---

[2] The difference between current prevalence and historical estimates.

[3] A European systematic review and meta-analysis of "transsexualism" prevalence studies by Arcelus *et al.* found an overall lower rate of 4.6 per 100,000. However, the review examined literature published from 1968 to 2014, before much of the recent surge in visibility and acceptance around transgender identities.

[4] Vrije Universiteit Amsterdam: https://www.ncbi.nlm.nih.gov/books/NBK544426/

One hypothesis for incongruity is that late in brain's development, when hormones flood the natal body and brain, the wrong hormones are present when used to establish connections and an overlay of sensitivity to them for later in life, such as puberty. The brain structures become established with the wrong hormonal overlay. The brain is not set up congruent with the physical structure of the body.

Some studies have indicated that the incongruent male's brain is more alike a female's brain in some structures and the incongruent female's brain is more alike a males' brain in some structures[5]. Whether these differences are at the root of gender incongruity or simply indicative of a biological difference is unknown.

Historically, the ratio of male to female gender incongruent had been between 70-80/30-20. In the last few years, the ratio is thought to be closer to 50/50, with the current prevalence figure above being 65/35.- about 2:1. The problem pointed out in Abigail Shrier's <u>Irreversible Damage</u>, that a significant increase in teen girls coming out trans, has flipped the ratio to 1:2, or closer to 30/70 male/female with no known medical reason for the change from historical averages.

One possible explanation for the greater prevalence of biological males being transsex: we all start from a biological foundation that is mostly female and our chromosomes make changes into 'male'. The mother's hormones DO pass into the blood of the fetus and under the right conditions - a significant increase in the mother's estrogen levels at the right time - can affect the development of the fetus. As the mother does not have a significant amount of testosterone there is less chance for this situation to affect a female fetus. How and why this situation would exist in biological females is probably associated with a significant drop in estrogen during a similar point in fetal development.

➢ *Transgender and Transsex Community Distinctions*

Media and political ideologues have confused and twisted our situation to further their own agendas. For the average person, trying to

---

[5] Gender Dysphoria: A Review Investigating the Relationship Between Genetic Influences and Brain Development https://www.ncbi.nlm.nih.gov/pmc/articles/PMC7415463/

find some clarity and understanding of what gender incongruity is and means for those with it, is an exercise in frustration.

For more than 50 years the term transsexual has been used both in the community and in the medical and legal communities to recognize a person with gender incongruity seeking medical treatment. Most older transsexuals people still prefer this term.

Among the younger generation, the term transsexual has a 'sexual' connotation that they find difficult to accept. The argument is that the term intersex does not have the 'ual' suffix and neither should transsex. Hard enough to gain acceptance of the change when 'trans' has become the singular term used to describe ALL gender non-conforming individuals.

The 'trans' community has two different groups. The transsex person believes gender is innate and immutable, that we are of a gender different than our birth biological/physical sex. We believe that those suffering such an incongruity suffer from gender dysphoria and need to medically transition to the other sex.

A transgender individual is someone that believes gender is fluid and can change over time. That there doesn't need to be dysphoria, they do not need to medically transition (usually), and they believe the assertion of an identity is sufficient cause to require society to recognize their identification.

There are transsex people that believe gender Is fluid, and transgender people that believe it is immutable. The groups are not mutually exclusive, generally. That being said, at the political level, where the community fights for various causes, the distinction becomes more pronounced.

The prominent community activists generally come from the transgender group. While they generally claim to speak for all types of gender non-conforming individuals, they do not.

This book comes from the transsex point of view. While there are many similarities of experiences between the two groups, generally during the teen years, the root differences are significant. To avoid many of the political, ideological, and societal debates, I will use transsex throughout the book when relevant but prefer gender incongruent to describe us.

*

If you are a parent with a child that has expressed gender incongruity, you are probably trying to figure out where this is all coming from. I hope the following helps. If someone in your life has told you they are gender incongruent (or any of the above terms), and you don't really understand what that means, I hope this gives you some insight.

---

[6] Differences between transgender and transsexual:
https://www.healthline.com/health/transgender/difference-between-transgender-and-transsexual

STARTING PREMISE

"When did we start letting three-year-olds decide what gender they are?" Bill Maher, celebrity

Gentlemen, you didn't DECIDE your gender to be male, you've always known you're male. Never questioned it; didn't even know to think something different. You just were. And that certainty is absolute. Ladies, same with you and being female – never more so than when you first started menses.

But for us, we never had that certainty, and we knew something was wrong from a very early age. Far earlier than you can imagine. This is not about emotions. Before you were aware that girls were not just different boys, or boys were not just different girls, before you were aware of the intrinsic (and explicit) differences, WE knew we were being put in with the wrong group.

What was wrong many couldn't articulate at the time, but we knew we were not the boys or girls our parents and others believed us to be.

Many ask, how do you know? *We feel it deep in our core knowledge of self. It is as fundamental as your feelings of male/female.*

How do you know you are a man/woman despite your biological/physical reality as a female/male? *It is a matter of comparison.*

Can you tell me what being a man/woman feels like? *The answer is that it is a matter of context.*

When a man asks what a woman feels like of an incongruent male, he lacks the context to understand the answer: *like a woman*. When a woman asks, the answer is: *like you*.

When a woman asks what a man feels like of an incongruent female, she lacks the context to understand the answer: *like a man*. When a man asks, the answer is: *like you*.

How do we **KNOW**? Different from that deep, core understanding of ourselves? We interact with peers and others and see how they act and react to circumstance; we compare those actions and reactions to our own and recognize that we fit more closely with the opposite biological sex. It doesn't mean we WANT to be there; it means we SHOULD be there. Does that mean there is a biological basis for gender and personality? Yes. The nature of a child is not learned; it is a function of their biological heritage. We, as children, recognize how others react and how we 'agree' or 'disagree' with them, where we fit.

This is not a one-time thing or a comparison to one person or even a group. This effort of comparison continues to happen over years. It happens across groups of known peers and strangers we meet and see in our daily experiences, in different environments such as school, church, shopping, and trips/vacations. For many it starts as soon as we begin interacting with others in (pre)school settings and continues into and past puberty.

You can't explain how or why you experience masculinity or femininity. You will point to your physical characteristics and claim it is obvious. Obvious only that you acknowledge a biological/physical foundation. But that foundation at times is disrupted during natal development.

*

Birth defects affect **1 in every 33 babies born in the United States each year.**[7]

> *My brother was born with muscular dystrophy. At least*
> *three of my parents' children were born with Type I*
> *osteogenesis imperfecta (brittle bone disease).*

That any pregnancy results in a healthy baby is a miracle. The statement that God doesn't make mistakes might be quite right, but human biology is quite fallible.

---

[7] CDC: https://www.cdc.gov/ncbddd/birthdefects/data.html, also see Appendix and John Hopkins: https://www.hopkinsmedicine.org/health/conditions-and-diseases/osteogenesis-imperfecta

About **10 to 20 percent** of known pregnancies end in miscarriage. But the actual number is likely higher because many miscarriages occur very early in pregnancy — before you might even know about a pregnancy.[8]

My mother had two of eight of her known pregnancies that ended in miscarriage. Her first, and her seventh.

Why do we think it is the physical sex that is wrong? Why can't it just be a mental defect? We can look at a person's body and determine its physical sex, we can look at the chromosomes and determine the biological sex, but we can't look at the brain (generally) and determine its gender. Some parts of the female and male brain do appear differently, but we don't know if those parts make us feel female or male. Are we, our body?

If you were to have an accident, or cancer and lost your gonads, would that change your sex? No. You'd still be a man, or woman, despite many people to whom it has happened, feeling not fully otherwise.

Is our sense of self separate from the physical? Try this: lay on your bed (if married or have a partner have them do so also). Lay your arms so they are not touching you and have the lights out. Without any physical evidence, without the senses of touch or sight, you still know whether you are a man or a woman.

Losing a body part doesn't change our brain. Damage to the brain can cause a perfectly healthy body part to cease functioning. A body part has no sense or awareness of self, that is reserved for the totality of self. But a child born without a foot or missing an arm doesn't really know they lack something until they begin to compare themselves and their life with others. It takes that comparison to understand they are different. It takes context.

You are more than your gonads. Your masculinity or femininity is not solely grounded there. It is in your head. There are feminine appearing men that are still quite clearly men. And masculine appearing women that are still quite clearly women. Except among those clearly intersex[9], your gonads define the physical aspect of your sex. But they are only one aspect of your self-identity. Your sense of self is what gives substance to the

---

[8] Mayo Clinic: https://www.mayoclinic.org/diseases-conditions/pregnancy-loss-miscarriage/symptoms-causes/syc-20354298
[9] Intersex generally applies to those born with both genitals, or undefined, or poorly developed genitals.

physical, psychologically. So, we have decided that, yes, for us, the brain is the root of self, and it is the body that is wrong.

People see your physical sex and almost always stop there. They have identified you as male or female. Occasionally, if you are a bit more androgynous, they will take a second look. If they still can't assign you to one of the two biological sexes, you will be 'othered'.

Othered simply means that people are unable to categorize you in ways that make them comfortable. Depending on the circumstances, they might simply move on. Others might stop and (hopefully not but all too often) confront you. They will demand clarification or claim you are misrepresenting yourself based on their analysis. They don't know your biological sex though almost all of us assume one based on what we **see**. Unless you have been tested, you probably don't even know your own chromosomal reality, regardless of your certainty.

Mostly, the medical community is comfortable treating your apparent physical sex as if you were congruent. Our gender identity is assumed unless we identify ourselves to others otherwise. Even if you identify as the opposite sex gender wise, the medical community has to treat your physical sex. Those born male do not menstruate, and those born female do not have a prostate.

Some have argued that incongruent females that state they are male, do menstruate. In the sense that they are physically female, they are incorrect. Those I have spoken to find menses to be a horrifying reminder of their incongruity and seek to stop them as soon as possible. Incongruent males often have the same revulsion about erections. Those making the arguments are making a political point, not stating a biological/physical sex fact.

Gender is not a spectrum. It is a binary state. We are a dimorphic species. Ignoring chromosomal abnormalities, we are either male (XY) or female (XX). These chromosomes guide our physical development. Let me qualify the first statement: gender is centered upon the biological binary state. Gender can have a range of expressions within each binary state. Females can express very feminine to very masculine; males can express very masculine to very feminine. But each is centered on the biological dimorphic. Note it is the expression that has a spectrum, not the root gender.

Sex is based on the biological, but our gender is how we understand our bodies. Gender expression is how we present ourselves to the outside world based on the totality of our experiences, understanding and desires to interact with society. Gender roles are the ways in which society expects men and women to act, based on culture expectations of the sexes.

Gender dysphoria is a medical condition based on the consequence of incongruity. It can be intense feelings of wrongness, of physical discomfort with oneself, or just the awareness something is wrong. We might not even necessarily recognize the connection between this experience and our sex at first, but as we compare ourselves to others, it becomes clearer. It starts at an early age and informs how we interact with the world.

When we are young it's so much worse because we are alone in our knowledge, and we don't know that anything can correct what is wrong. We know we are wrong, but if we tell people, no one believes us. It doesn't go away, but it often does vary in intensity. Life gets in the way of us being in our head all the time. Some may appear normal to family, with occasional odd moments that are ignored, while others are faced with debilitating anxiety and depression.

---

[10] Journal of Clinical Endocrinology & Metabolism: https://academic.oup.com/jcem/article/101/12/4532/2765003
[11] NIH: https://medlineplus.gov/genetics/condition/46xx-testicular-difference-of-sex-development/#frequency
[12] Science Direct: https://www.sciencedirect.com/topics/psychology/gender-identity

The brain structure is set by the time we are born. We are what we are going to be by that time. We can choose many different ways to live our lives, but we enter them with a brain and chromosome structure we can't change[13]. There are many things that I think are brain structure dependent that people think are 'choices'.

NO ONE wakes up one morning and 'decides' they would rather be the opposite sex[14]. This is a complex issue that begins very early in life and continues until there is no personal choice but to make, the unfortunately public, transition to the opposite sex.

WE KNOW that we cannot change our chromosomal reality. We will die as we were born, chromosomally[15]. However, for most of us, we can adapt by changing our physical and hormonal state. We can self-express ourselves in a way that is no different than those born into the correct sex.

If you cannot imagine how such a thing could be possible, consider how hard it is for us to live with the incongruity from our earliest memories. We don't want this. We wouldn't wish this on our worst enemies. And we will have enemies, many throughout all the phases and times of our lives. Many will not even know us but just SEE us and attack us, vocally and too often physically. Some will be family members and 'friends' trying to save us from some perceived corruption.

What follows is a rough timeline of our thoughts and issues from our earliest years through to adulthood, transition and beyond.

---

[13] Brains can be damaged, causing minor to extreme personality changes.

[14] Yes, there are people that state exactly that. They however do not meet any medical criteria recognized as transsex.

[15] It is common in the US, and a few other places, for people to claim that by identifying as our correct gender, we claim to be of the other chromosomal sex. It is on its face false. Doing so places those of us that are gender incongruent in a box too easily dismissed.

CHILDHOOD

- THE FIRST YEAR

We recognize our parents and siblings early in our first year. Doesn't matter if we have physical issues, we just exist and these people, who we can distinguish from others, are in our daily existence. Our days are full of stimuli, sleep and growth. We lack a sense of self or understanding of our bodies. But our bodies do react to internal and external stimuli, usually instinctually.

Children don't yet understand the terms man, woman, boy or girl. They are just part of a group that we eventually term, family. We don't understand gender yet even if it appears that our choices are consistent with expectations.

If we are born with a birth defect, at this point, we could make no comparison even if we could be aware of it. The lack of a foot or arm, for example, doesn't change our behavior, we simply act as if the absence is irrelevant – because it is to us. You, as parents, might make comparisons and try to adapt but we as children are just happy to be with you and learn about, well, everything.

Those with severe medical issues obviously have different first months but even then, those children have no comparison – they are just dealing with their lives as they unfold. Parents are the ones trying to adapt to expectations and to reality and it can be excruciating. The children don't know that their life is heartbreak to all that know them. They have no comparison, no understanding of self. But they know the love they are shown, or not shown.

As that first-year progresses, we become more aware of "others" and our very limited physical world. Our concept of self begins to grow but it is still far from being able to compare ourselves to others. Watch a child that is exposed to a mirror for the first time. They will not recognize themselves. It takes time for us to recognize that the thing we see in the mirror is in fact our physical self.

How many times have we heard parents and family members talk about the nature of the newborn? Happy, picky, fussy, interested and even unhappy. The nature of a child, a composite of both their genetics and the development of their brain, provides a foundation of self that will take time to express itself fully. As these innate qualities become more established and more clearly expressed, reactions to others and the environment improve and begin to be consistent.

When aspects of that nature encompass more than one set of expectations, people that encounter the child can misunderstand. On rare occasions strangers may misgender male children as "cute" or "beautiful" girls or female children as "handsome" boys. Parents will be embarrassed and quick to correct them. This does not mean a child is incongruent.

This nature persists as the child grows. These are not learned personality traits but rather innate qualities. Those natural traits form the basis of the personality that develops as a child grows, and their environment and experiences add to their personality development.

Behaviors can be enhanced, diminished, or modified by our environment and how we interact with others. What do I mean by modified? My mother was born left-handed, in Ireland, in the 1930's. She attended a religious school and they literally, with a ruler, beat left-handedness out of her. It takes enormous effort to break the innate nature. Is that really what society wants to do to transsex - brutalize them into conformity?

One of the things we see develop with even very young children are preferences, in food choices and in people. But 'new' people do not always provoke negative responses, so it is not JUST 'new' person preference for some people and not others. Some people believe that we sense some aspect of others that we respond to, positively or negatively. In my opinion, that is akin to our almost instant recognition of someone that we know and is often but not exclusively gendered.

These preferences reflect the child's nature and natural traits and are part of personality development. It is easy to see aspects of the child's personality get expressed because they have little ability to hold it back. But aspects that are outside adult expectations are often dismissed as phases by parents. They should not be dismissed as they can often foreshadow future development.

By focusing on expectations, rather than acknowledging those aspects as they are, parents begin to consider restrictions or modifications on their child's natural behaviors if they fail to conform. This will lead to further complications soon.

Memories form at the earliest age. But memories, figuratively, are locked in files, in filing cabinets, in rooms, in a large building we have no way to find. We have no way to access them because we lack a context or reference point.

> *My earliest memory was of me on the kitchen table screaming my head off because my mom and aunt were trying to remove some tape from between my legs. I always assumed it was after I came out of the hospital at age 5.*

> *It wasn't until I was in my thirties when my mom and I were discussing the above memory that she asked me to describe the kitchen. The description fit our first apartment, not our first house five years later. The situation was just before my christening, just after being released from the hospital, when I was ~10-12 days old.*

> *That memory, well beyond what most people can recall, was so vivid because of that later event that created a reference point.*

– YEAR TWO AND THREE

Children are introduced to more people and as they are able, will play and interact with other children. They form into groups consistent with their nature, and a pattern of behavior consistent with their group. Generally, but not always, a group of boys and girls will segregate themselves according to sex.

This is part of the context noted earlier. The innate qualities include awareness of the emotional state of others and a recognition of compatible qualities. Events cause those qualities to be expressed.

"WHAT DOES THAT EVEN MEAN? BE A GUY, BE A GIRL? ONCE YOU GET PAST THE OBVIOUS PHYSICAL NATURE OF IT, IT IS ALL ABOUT CONFORMING TO THE EXPECTATIONS OF SOCIETY."

THE WAY YOU SEE ME, MAERYN LAMONTE 2022

When a child expresses behavior stereotypically seen as inconsistent with their physical appearance, such as a boy playing with girls or dolls, or a girl playing with boys or trucks, parents or other adults that are present may remove the child or reposition them with the "appropriate" group. But that may confuse the child. It is important for parents to recognize that this is innate behavior, not learned or caused by the environment.

There can be lots of reasons for their behavior, it does not necessarily mean the child is gender incongruent. It is context expressed; the child's nature reacting to the environment and circumstances.

It should not be ignored or dismissed. Behavioral analysis works for most of us that are quite similar. Where it fails is amongst those that are not like the rest. Early childhood behaviors are not always clear explicit choices of the child.

Incongruent children diverge from their peer group very early. Those innate natures are noticed by peers almost as soon as their interactions start.

Think of two infants, under two, meeting for the first time. They can get along great or not. It's too soon for most behaviors to develop, too early for adults to impose behaviors. All that the children can go on is the environment they are in and their nature. And those natures can be compatible, or not.

Putting children into mixed groups and allowing them to express themselves will help parents and other adults learn the nature of their child and help them develop. When adults are embarrassed by the child's behavior(s), two things will happen:

1) The methods used to "correct" the child will become increasingly harsh.
2) The child will learn that certain behaviors result in punishments even if they don't understand why. It will be confusing because the behavior is part of their nature. This response will be the beginning of alienation from the parents.

You might argue that such behavior is not likely in kids this young, but it is a process that starts very early. A stronger willed child will push back or continue their behavior despite the adult intervention until the parent restricts opportunities for the "unexpected" behavior to occur. This works until the child begins to interact with others outside the presence of their parents, such as at a nursery, with babysitters, or in preschool. Even if parents are not restrictive, other adults may be. In such a case, alienation with parents may take a different perspective: why are you making me be with 'those' people?

− YEAR FOUR THROUGH SIX

Having children that can remember at early ages is rare. My brother claims not to remember anything of our childhood and even my other siblings remember very little from before the age of ten. By "early ages is rare" with regard to memories, I am focused on pre-5. Most seem to have a few memories from ages 6-8 with most people recalling ages 9/10 forward. How can people learn from children unable to articulate what is going on in their heads? Especially when their thoughts are rare, unique, or unexpected.

Researchers work to eliminate non-relevant variables, but children are learning machines. They are very observant and excellent readers of body language, even at fairly early ages.

> *With my memories, often detailed and including my emotional state at the time, I am concerned that my current self is influencing my perceptions of my past self.*

Children articulate facts, as they understand them, to the extent they have the vocabulary to do so.

There is a belief that when children say phrases like, "I am a princess" and "I am a girl" that they must be saying the same thing. That there is an inability to distinguish between make-believe and reality and that we should not put any emphasis on the latter. But children understand the distinction fairly early and at about the same time that gender identity begins to be expressed. Children know the difference.[16]

Adults correct them when they make statements that the adult knows are inaccurate. A male child stating they are a girl is obviously inaccurate. But is it? For the adults, again, it seems obvious. They would and do assume they are trying to say "feel like" or "want to be" because most adults have never considered the possibility of incongruity. And of course, what does a three-year-old know?

---

[16] Make-believe and fact: https://news.utexas.edu/2006/11/27/young-children-learn-to-distinguish-between-fact-and-fiction-research-at-university-of-texas-at-austin-finds/

Context is vital. The child is not saying, this is my sex, these are my chromosomes. What they are expressing is their understanding of self. The child compares themselves and how they relate to others, to their understanding of how others are relating to others.

> *At age five I suffered several injuries over the summer months that caused a hydrocele[17]; were they self-inflicted? Attempts to damage what I was born with? Or was it just a very active, somewhat clumsy, kid having a series of accidents? There is no way for me to know, but because I was subconsciously aware something was wrong, I can't dispute it.*

With no context for someone else's behavior, you can't assume you know what they're thinking or even their emotions. When an adult is faced with a child that is acting outside of societal (or even parental) expectations, the adult will apply their own understanding to the situation. But that understanding may not be relevant.

For many therapists, this potential issue is often mitigated by their education, experience, and evaluation of circumstance, or potentially made worse. This could be changing, but I have seen examples of adults assuming generalized statements from their children including words such as "feel like," or "want to be," as statements of fact. In my opinion, it seems like the pendulum has swung too far the other way in some circumstances.

Between four and seven is when the experts say gender is formed[18]. I think this is incorrect. I believe gender to be innate, but it takes time for the outward expression of it to manifest itself in a way that is recognizable to adults. The more socially isolated and gender-segregated a child is, the later it appears, because they lack context (opportunities to compare).

That could mean, depending on the circumstances, a child may not show any incongruity until nine, ten or even later. Whereas a child in an open and diverse environment may show an incongruity much earlier.

It is what adults do when a child shows any incongruity that determines the mental health of their child for the rest of their life.

---

[17] Hydrocele: A fluid-filled sac around a testicle, often first noticed as swelling of the scrotum.
[18] See Appendix for a discussion on the expert opinion.

It only takes one aggressive episode from an adult for a child to learn to withdraw from their parents and/or other adults. Parents often will be sharp with a child over behaviors the parent deems risky or dangerous. Things like running with a sharp object or climbing on furniture, for example. If the child repeats the behavior, the parent's responses will be sharper. Children don't always equate the sharp response with the risk; they think they are wrong (rather than the action). Watch a child react in those situations and it tends to be pretty clear that they think the parent feels differently towards them. How the parent acts and the words chosen can have a significant impact.

When the behavior is gender oriented, it is the 'self' that is believed to be wrong, not the behavior. So, the child pulls back across a broad spectrum of behaviors.

I am not a fan of behavioral analysis with regard to young(er) children. Context and understanding are inferred. I am sure, as the above shows, that that practice tends to work well with the vast majority of kids. But the internalization that happens when gendered behavior is involved is what I am focusing on. My parents didn't specifically restrict my behaviors on gendered grounds, but in all of the situations I can recall when growing up, my parents put me with other boys when there was a gender choice.

Also, as indicated elsewhere, my parents' use of punishment was very act specific – they didn't call me bad, just what I did bad. It was an important distinction and one that I used with my daughter much later. Still, I learned that my thoughts about being a girl were not going to be welcomed or accepted.

"That is for your sister, not you, you're a boy."

Peers enforce conformity in their own ways, often equally harshly and it takes only one negative response from peers to teach us to keep our nature from them or withdraw all together.

"Why do you want to play with GIRLS?!?"

Those that learn to pretend, or hide their nature, will seem to have "gotten over the phase" but that is not true at all. This is not to say that some children who are unsure about themselves won't come to a natural conclusion and conform to normal expectations. It happens in the majority of cases. The apparent similarity of behavior sometimes belies the actual reality.

Outside settings

Nursery, pre-school, and pre-kindergarten expand the circumstances for children to express their nature. Girls play with girls doing girl things and boys play with boys doing boy things. And adults supervising them often encourage this division, either explicitly or implicitly.

I was 4 when my sister was born, and I was exposed to an anatomy different from my own. I don't think I made any conscious comparison but by five there were tiny signs my mother was able to, much later, put into context.

My first friends in the neighborhood were girls. I did not go to any babysitting or pre-schools. Kindergarten was my first exposure to alternate adult supervision. I have snippets or memories from kindergarten and first grade, but I don't remember any friends from school.

There were two boys nearby. The boy that lived across the street made it pretty clear he did not want to interact with me despite our mother's friendship with each other. The other had a sister that I got along with much better.

In recent years, many early childhood development schools have tried to eliminate gender separating behaviors. The consequence, for the vast majority, is an opening up of experiences. But when the artificial lack of a divide is removed, the children will often revert to a 'natural gender segregation'. Natural qualities will encourage children into "like" groups even when the biology/physical attributes cause friction. We see girls do things and everyone is fine, we do it and all hell breaks out. We don't understand why it is right for girls (or boys) and not for us? Except that it provokes a strongly negative response.

For the few with incongruity, it will confuse them if their parents have been forcefully segregating behaviors. Many will flourish in such a school environment but get shocked back at home with negative consequences. Parents will demand the schools conform to their expectations for their child. What is acceptable or unacceptable behavior becomes a function of the environment. Home, school, and work - environments that will persist for decades.

For more standard schools, it will not only be adults that enforce the gender divide, it will be the children themselves. Often girls wanting to play with boys will be allowed, and even in some cases welcomed. Boys wanting to play with girls, however, will often be excluded and rejected by both groups.

Most children recognize they have differences, and a few will speak openly about it. As it is at home and now with peers in school. Peers will impose their own understanding of appropriate behaviors upon other children. Children that act contrary to expectations will be 'othered'. We often learn that we can't be what comes naturally to us and because of that alienation, love and friendship are not available to us, or are limited.

By five or six the gender incongruent child will know two things:

1) They are different than other kids; and
2) The need to hide it from parents, other adults, and their peers.

The question "why?" will occupy time in their heads for years. And one possible answer will cause more damage than anyone could predict.

• Why?

The first time I was bullied was by that boy from across the street at about age five. The first time I was beaten up was at age seven.

If you have ever had children, why is a word, and a question, that you were answering sometimes numerous times per hour, for years! "Why?" has been asked by every single person since the word was invented.

Today, we have the internet, and we get an answer to why almost any time we ask, even if that answer is grossly wrong. But there are whys that can't be answered, even when the question is from a very young child.

When younger:

Why am I a freak? Why can't I be like other boys/girls? Why did God do this to me? Am I being punished?

When older:

Why am I this way? Why can't I be normal? Why does everything seem so wrong when I do what is expected?

The question gets asked because we recognize that we are not being treated the same way others that we identify with are being treated. We can't or won't be allowed to play with other girls (because everyone **KNOWS** we are boys), or other boys (because everyone **KNOWS** we are girls). We don't understand so, like in our more formative years of two and three, we ask why. When there is no answer that makes sense to us, parents get frustrated with the questioning, it gets dropped and the question turns inward.

When does the question, in this context, begin? For some as early as three or four. These kids are often the most expressive of their incongruity. They are the ones at ages three or four that outright declare to parents and any other adults, "I'm a girl" or "I'm a boy".

But many, if not most gender incongruent children **know** we are different within a year or two of starting school[19]. There is just too much evidence for us to ignore even if we don't know or understand.

By the time I was 6 or 7, I knew I was "different". Although it appeared, subconsciously, I knew earlier.

That I was different was beyond question. Every time boys would do or say things that I couldn't understand, separated me from "them". Why did they behave that way; why did they say those things? I had no idea and at six no chance to understand.

All I knew was that I looked at other girls and knew I wanted to be with them, not with the boys who were increasingly antagonistic towards me. I just tried to keep my distance and my head down.

When the question fails to provoke an answer from the all-knowing parents and adults, and we just accept we are not going to get an answer, the wishing, dreaming, and praying begins.

Knowing we are different isn't a positive. We want to be like everyone else. We want to be normal while also wanting to be what we wish and pray for.

At four, five or six we are aware, but don't understand that what we are feeling is at odds with our reality. We express ourselves the way we can: we should be a girl/boy but obviously to everyone we are not, so we wish, or pray for change. It will take years and a better understanding and vocabulary to articulate what we understood intrinsically: we were born wrong. It creates a type of split personality. Can't we be normal? Can't we be the "other"?

We spend years in our heads trying to answer why and figuring out how to keep people from finding out our secret. The internet helps kids

---

[19] One study [Division of Urology, Cedars-Sinai Medical Center] showed that, on average, study participants reported their earliest memory of gender dysphoria between the ages of 4 and 6 years old. By the age of 7, most study participants could remember experiencing some feelings of gender dysphoria.

learn they are not alone; that there is a name for what is wrong, but we eventually find out, NO ONE has the answer to why.

"Why can't I be normal?" becomes the unanswerable question that all interaction with others is tainted by. If we are bullied, even when our secret is unknown, we believe it to be because of the "secret" and because parents/adults either directly or indirectly call such "secret" bad, too often, we consider the bullying to be **DESERVED** punishments.

> *I believe because I felt safe at home and religion, while present, wasn't day-to-day determinant, I did not internalize the bullying. My parent's punishment was directed to specific behavior, so it had a specific context. Why the bullying was happening was still a question, but I never **blamed** myself for it.*

*

Note: It is important for me to stress going into the next section that I am not faulting any particular religion. I have found very accepting people in every religion. I am speaking about specific people with a religious conviction that may or may not conform to the religion's teachings.

Those within a religious environment at home have a harder time because we get a name for why: we are sinning. If, for some reason, our secret is learned, guessed at, or even used simply as an accusation, the abuse tends to be worse from individuals that assert:

1) "God doesn't make mistakes."
2) "God made you male/female."

Obviously, with 1 out of every 33 children born with a birth defect, #1 above would seem to either be wrong, or their interpretation of God is very cruel. And #2 is true of biological and physical sex, but maybe not gender. But intersex can call even that into question.

In the worst situations, we are seen as evil. In these cases, we must be punished. And this alienates us deeper and further from parents, family, other adults, and peers. Those punishments, the increasingly harsh methods parents and other adults use to force conformity can border on extreme, and even criminal.

Over the years the child will conform, if only to preserve themselves. Once a parent knows the incongruity exists, because our nature cannot be hidden perfectly, it will always be a factor in the relationship. It is from this group that we see parents kick their child out of the house.[20]

As noted, I am not speaking in regard to any particular religion, but rather about how people interpret those religions in their day to day lives and how they apply their perception of their religion's beliefs to the gender incongruent. There is no option in that environment other than internalizing the belief that our nature is evil or corrupt. And it destroys a person's sense of self.

*

Every negative event is filtered through our knowledge that the secret others us, even when no one else knows. We don't know why we are how we are, but we can't seem to separate it from every bad thing that happens to us. In the absence of a concrete answer to why, we try every other explanation.

We can't seem to stop being ourselves, even when we try to figure out how to behave correctly. We mimic our peers or try to conform but our treatment at the hands of parents, adults and peers is a betrayal of us. A betrayal by parents that are supposed to love, not hurt, by other adults in our lives that are supposed to be safe, not dangerous, and our peers who are supposed to be friends, not bullies and enemies.

The further we withdraw, the further we pull back in fear, shame, and guilt. We are wrong, bad, evil. And the more we hide, the greater our alienation. Like a hamster wheel we can't get off.

We go to bed hoping, wishing that we wake up changed. We wish at birthdays, at Christmas, at every shooting star. We pray to the God of our

---

[20] According to the 2015 Transgender Survey, 8% of trans teens were kicked out of their birth family home. People of color were kicked out of the house at higher rates, with Middle Eastern respondents (17%) being twice as likely, and American Indian (14%), Black (12%), Latino/a (11%), multiracial (11%), and Asian (9%) respondents.

religion. We offer anything to make us normal – but most often it is a normal of the other sex.

When nothing changes, we call into question everything we are being told about wishing, about religion, about faith. We wake unchanged with a sense of hopelessness that infects everything. Adults see this but can only use their own context, their own understanding of reality to try and help their child (or punish them). Small hints of our inherent nature are either ignored, dismissed as inconsequential or worse, used as evidence of our bad or evil nature.

They will try to talk to us, try to get us to open up about what is bothering us, but we have already learned that they don't believe us, they will be angry that we are imagining or make-believing, and so we will try to beg off, distract, or just wait them out. We can't talk to them because they won't do anything to change our circumstances. But that situation sets a tone for the rest of our days.

"Why?" can't be answered by therapy. Therapists and parents want to change the question to "why don't you want to be a boy/girl?" Because we are not. We know this despite all the physical evidence to the contrary. That no one wants to consider our innate nature confuses and angers us. For the majority of us, this has become the root of many mental health issues for years.

When you live with the incongruity, it affects every relationship, but most importantly, our sense of self. We recognize that we physically are wrong, and the distress begins so, so early in our lives. That distress is gender dysphoria.

Medically, gender dysphoria is significant distress with one's own body. Every incongruent person is different with regard to the intensity of their dysphoria. From indifference and occasional intense desire for change to severe 'hatred' and clinical depression.

Those with milder forms will often appear no different than their peers. And parents will assume they 'grew out ' of whatever incongruity was expressed. We didn't, it got worse, but we just got better at trying to fit in.

– YEAR SEVEN THROUGH TEN

• Acceptance, until…

For the next several years, a type of routine sets in. For me, the bad days of bullying were offset as I had a stable and loving home but for many, if not most, bad days outnumber the good.

School and home life, if stable, could be predictable. Most make one or two friends with one thing in common: we are 'othered'.

For me, my dysphoria was worse when I had a bunch of good days because I had more time and energy to devote to my 'whys'. Bad days made me focus on those, mostly external things.

I was luckier than most in that my dysphoria was not crippling. I never hated myself and the early bullying was pretty tame, relatively. When the bullying got much more intense in seventh and eighth grades (11-13 yrs. old), I never blamed myself or my nature.

Being 'othered' is almost universal amongst those with gender incongruity. Even when we learn to hide, or repress, our feelings, our nature still leaks through, and the incongruities confuse people. Kids can be brutal when someone doesn't fit in.

Somewhere between five and nine, most of us have accepted that we are different, that we need to hide it, and we figure out how to at least survive in our day-to-day lives. There might be days when all appears fine, even normal. We might go weeks where the question of why is mostly in the background. We go to school, learn what we are being taught, learn we are not thinking the same way as our biological sex peers; We learn to keep our 'secret' tightly held. But we are not functioning the same as our peers. We are withdrawn (for safety's sake), and parents are at a loss how to deal with us, if they are even paying attention. (Yes, many of us become cynical early).

We function. Some of us do. Sort of. We hear people say: you're a freak; you're weird; you're a pervert; you are a bad person; no one loves or wants a freak. We don't know how to fight it, how to rebut them. When those things are said to us by peers, and too often by parents and siblings, we internalize the words, it becomes a voice in our heads we can't avoid.

We reject ourselves. We accept we are different but can't accept what we are. This lack of self-acceptance becomes ingrained by the voices from outside, and unfortunately the voice inside. It is a lack of acceptance that will persist for years. So, a significant portion eventually become involved in alcohol or drugs to try and quiet those external, and internal voice. At some point, for many, depression sets in.

It is not just depression. The external voices cause us to question everything we know and understand, in our limited way at this age. If we are bad, evil, or a freak, then we deserve the bad things happening to us. And we can't allow ourselves to accept anything good. There is no control over what we are feeling, so we will try anything to get some control, or to purge ourselves of the thoughts. Eating disorders are a common way to punish; cutting becomes a way to dull the pain; even rudimentary attempts at suicide though they may not be recognized as such.

Of course, so I say, these are symptoms of gender dysphoria, of the root gender incongruence. IF parents or a school recognize depression and seek out clinical help, it almost certainly tries to treat the wrong thing; because we won't talk about what is really happening in our heads. We've learned to protect ourselves at the cost of almost anything. And depression is just a symptom. Treating it is useless[21]. But as depression and other issues persist, increasingly severe treatment is used causing all kinds of additional issues. Frankly, such clinical treatment is no better than the self-treatment done by kids using drugs and alcohol.

How can I make such a statement? I am not a trained therapist or clinical physician, but the experience I do have is that I have met and talked to hundreds of us. Even across geographic and demographic lines, the similarities are astounding. Such treatment fails over and over because it is not focused on the actual problem – our gender incongruity.

---

[21] Obviously, treating the depression ISN'T useless. But it can't be resolved as long as the underlying gender dysphoria remains.

Many find acceptance in counterculture, not because it reflects what we are, but because there are 'others' that can provide them with some kind of protection. Of course, this often confuses the parents even more but for us, it tends to hide the real issue (sometimes even from ourselves). We have successfully distracted everyone from what is really going on within us. But like alcohol and drugs, it doesn't fix us. It doesn't answer the question "why?". All we've done is build a fortress around our incongruity, one that gets bigger and stronger as the years progress.

Why do some of us have these issues and not others? After many discussions, it seems to come down to home environment, and parents. Parents that are upset over our differences create, whether they seek to or not, a climate of fear. Fear that we will be punished not in response to an action, but because of our very nature, if it happens to leak out. A father finding a son more interested in stereotypical girl toys instead of stereotypical boy toys, or a mother that finds her daughter rough housing, playing sports, and hating dresses. Their reactions, often very vocal or even physical, teach us to withdraw and hide as much as possible. This climate alienates us from family and causes us to lack a 'safe space'. Mentally, we check out. We can't win.

From the point we acknowledge to ourselves that we are different, and we understand, even in a rudimentary way, how we are different, until the ages of 10 to 12, we are in a general holding pattern. At least if we have a nominally stable life of home and school (and/or church). We accept our standing and for days, weeks, months, and years; we survive. If we do not have that stability, we lose our own mental stability. We bounce around different attempts to find a solution, a safe space.

Many parents will try to ignore the occasional lapses of hiding our nature. The girls are called tomboys and are often encouraged and accepted by other boys and even parents. The boys, however, get called vile slurs. They are ostracized, bullied and even the adults are quick to tell us to 'man up', or 'grow a thicker skin'. I often heard the phrase 'boys will be boys' used as an excuse for the bullying I received.

The casual acceptance of bullying by teachers and school administrators is frightening. Even in places with "zero tolerance" programs, they barely scratch the surface of bullying behavior. It is all too easy for kids to pick on others and if supervision is tight, ostracization can carry the same othering result.

• Essay : Bullying

Let me make the following assertion clear: I am identifying groups, not individuals. I have known considerate kids in every one of the categories below who treat everyone in ways that we can all appreciate and hope to emulate. Fortunately, they are not rare. But for every one of the best there are three or four that fall well short of the ideal. But it is not just one group that has issues.

Bullying in school is universal (at least if I can trust both individual stories and the stories shown in the media). Adults seem unable to do anything, even when they demand zero tolerance programs. I believe in part because too many of them seem to accept and indirectly encourage it. But it is our peers that cause so much damage.

What follows was part of an essay for school kids and was not specifically about gender incongruity. I saw the divisions in my school years, the years of my siblings, and even 30 years later in my daughter's schools. It is partly a popularity ranking but also an academic one. It is a discussion for school kids to understand their part in bullying and in some ways, to help prevent it. And for parents to recognize they seldom get the whole picture.

The Popular Kids:

The most popular kids are usually the 'best looking', at least as determined by the students in the top half of those thought to be good looking. Those in the bottom half seldom have a voice in the matter. It is not just appearances that determine this group, but participation in school activities such as sports and school sanctioned groups. Occasionally it will include the smartest kids but rarely the top academic performers. The popular kids WILL usually be in the top 5% academically for a host of reasons but I consider family demands on academic performance to be the most important.

These are not usually thought of as being bullies, they do not need to bully to assert themselves higher on the social ladder. But often enough their attitudes can set the tone and opinions of those around them that do bully.

Kids in this group also face enormous social pressures: from families looking to show off their top-level children; families that derive some social standing from their children's accomplishments; teachers that derive social standing from having the popular kids in their classes; and from other kids in the group.

There is also the problem of these kids trying to live up to the expectations of their parents that are often unrealistic, and it leaves the kids, despite their success, believing they have failed. None of this excuse the bullying of others. Their bullying is seldom actual physical contact or specific words. Kids that sneer or look down upon others is a form of bullying. It intimidates, it denigrates, it demeans others. Someone that does not have the most current fashions, or the best social behavior are often targeted – opportunistically – with derision.

Kids in this group occasionally are ignorant of their own behavior, caught in their own situations, they reflect their parent's attitudes without thought or consideration. If you think others lack the appropriate social graces, or wear clothing that is "no better than Walmart", then you are part of the problem. Not everyone can afford the best clothes, not everyone has had the same opportunities in social situations, not everyone has a safe, stable, successful home front.

Rarely but not as infrequently as we might hope, there are popular kids that abuse their position actively, personally and with malicious intent.

Right now, most of the student body know who the bullies are amongst the popular kids. They will not tell adults who could do something because the top kids' popularity protects them from the predation of others and from actions from teachers. Teachers are not immune from social stratification in the school. If the popular kids like a teacher, that teacher derives social standing from their status. Those teachers often excuse and ignore when popular kids engage in the same behavior that they often quickly and strongly punish those lower on the ladder for engaging in. Administrators are likewise loath to take any action against the popular kids, often noting it is not just the kids, but their parent's social status that can make them endangered. For while teachers and administrators are often 'at the top' in a school, they are seldom in such a position outside the school.

If we could have a perfectly anonymous poll about who the popular kids are and which are bullies, outsiders would probably be aghast. But it would surprise NO ONE within the school.

What can you do?

Popular kids have enormous social capital within the school. They can stop a bully in their tracks. They can go to teachers and administrators and support anti-bullying efforts. They can ostracize those that bully from their social circles. Some do so. Most don't for many of the reasons noted above. It should not be left up to the students to do the job of the teachers and administrators (or parents), yet it should not be a responsibility abdicated to them. If you know your friends bully – tell them, it is unacceptable and add consequences to the assertion.

Tier 2

These are the kids that are friends or group associates of the popular kids. Often, they consider themselves part of the popular kids because of their association with them, but they are the 'enforcers' of the popular kid's attitudes rather than being the source of those attitudes. These kids take the sneers and snobby looks and translate them into actual physical confrontations. They will come up to others and actively call out "lower caste" kid's appearances or characteristics as inappropriate. Participation in school activities with the popular kids is often sufficient for them to consider themselves at the top of the heap.

They are usually as untouchable as the popular kids because of their associations. I hate to note that it is these kids that corrupt the system in such a way that no one trusts it to protect them. Everyone sees their bullying behavior and the inaction of teachers and administrators to stop it. Further, even the popular kids will not stop them because they derive social

---

[22] Sheffield Hallam University: https://shura.shu.ac.uk/10145/1/Formby_-_Rotherham_final_report_2015.pdf

status from the 'adoring tier' and to see their own behaviors enforced encourages more of it.

This is also the group where we find the best kids, those that are near the top in popularity, academics and who watch out for, or are friends with the targets of active bullies. They are often immune from attacks, but they can also be ignorant of them. Believing that others are like them, kind and compassionate, they often fail to see the marginal bullying behavior in others. They have social standing to mitigate bullying, but they cannot be everywhere all the time. They have their own social pressures from their peers and their parents. Parents and teachers that often engage in their own form of bullying against this group by noting they 'just don't quite measure up but if they could just put A LITTLE MORE EFFORT, they could be more….popular...smarter...'

Bullies will avoid active antagonism of others while in the presence of the tier two kid because the tier two kid is PERSONALLY popular. They do not derive their popularity from social status but because of their good personalities.

In the top half of the school, you will find the greatest divide between bully and non-bully in this group. Often the differences will be so stark as to stun.

Again, if we could have a perfectly anonymous poll, there would be overwhelming numbers for each side and few surprises on the bullying side.

What can you do?

You have the greatest influence in the school, even greater in many regards than the popular kids or teachers because most of the student body looks up to you. Of course, that influence can be used well or poorly so it is up to you to choose. Do not be afraid to use your influence and social capital against bullies. And if you are one of those enforcers of the status ladder, stop. It does not improve your standing and it will only hurt you in the long run.

Middle Ground

These are the kids that usually do not bully, nor are directly bullied. They lack the social standing to derive benefit from the top and are not so far out of alignment with the social standings as to face derision from others.

Their academic level keeps them from being the focus of teachers and administrators and parents are 'just happy they are succeeding'. They don't doom the academic curves, don't cause problems for teachers, and keep to themselves and often small social circles of like students.

Their social status likewise doesn't disrupt the upper tiers and doesn't offend the sensibilities sufficiently to cause others to denigrate them. Their small social circles tend to provide some insulation from the effects of any bullying.

You won't find many advocates for others in this group except for those within their own social groups. They don't attend the same classes, don't engage in school activities, and are all but invisible to the teachers and administrators. No one encourages them to be more or do better. Not even their parents. They simply get along and do what is required and don't disturb the peace, anyone's peace.

What can you do?

There is little this group can do to change any dynamics except to be open to including others from lower groups to join in with their social circles. It will protect a few from overt bullying. But there will be too many, too diverse, to fit into those circles.

The Bottom Rungs

The bottom of the social hierarchy, and often the bottom of the academic one also. Although, the truly academic bottom is full of the kids that have given up, who have been given up on – by teachers, administrators, and parents – and those that have a difficult time in traditional academic settings. The bullies here are often the opportunistic bullies that harm others whenever they get a chance. Some, including myself, believe they are being harmed themselves and too often it is true. Others are just lashing out at available targets.

But the majority are the 'othered'. Those that do not fit into the established societal roles that school settings seem to create. Up until recently, the gender incongruent often found themselves here often in spite of their academic ability or because it was compromised by their dysphoria and social status.

Where possible, many find a friend or couple that can provide some buffer from the worst of the harassment. But no one can avoid bullies ALL the time and they are caught alone by singular bullies or often the bully and friends. Picking on the smallest, the lone kid, is a stereotypical hallmark of the bully for a reason. It happens. A lot.

Teachers and administrators all but ignore this group's picked on situations because they are 'out of sight and out of mind'. They are not social kids, they are not the academic performers, they are the quiet, unassuming with their head down trying to just get through the day, kids and it is easy to miss them, and what is happening to them. But intervention here often backfires as bullies always blame their target for adult intervention against them.

What can you do?

Keep parents and other adults informed about what is going on. Try and build a social circle. Both of which would already exist if they could easily. Both are difficult for those in this group, unless you want to give up and join those that have already done so. Resist giving up because things do change.

*

Bullying from our peers prevents us from establishing the type of social interactions necessary for our teen years and adult relationships. Bullying from adults, implicitly or explicitly, causes us to fear adults and too often reject any adult authority. We have learned not to trust them. And finally, the words and deeds of parents, rejecting us (by rejecting 'othered'), leaves us without help or support.

Bullying is near universal. It happens in every school, across geo and demographics. More so in some than in others. Where education has broken down, it happens to teachers almost as often as it does to students.

> *I dealt with it from five until fourteen in varying degrees and*
> *regularity. My secret was never a factor; I was 'othered'*
> *despite the lack of knowledge by others. It ended for me*
> *when I finally fought back at 15. I was scared stiff when I did*

that they would attack harder, but they backed off.
Thankfully. It doesn't always happen that way.

– Acceptance, until… continued

For those of us that obtain some mental stability, we live on. Our parents, siblings and peers just accept us, (or ignore us), as we do, and nothing changes. The question of why is continuously on our mind and it remains stubbornly unanswered in all of its forms. We live in our heads. We tend to be quieter than others, many of us are good students but teachers recognize we are not trying, not reaching our potential. Those that have issues created by a lack of safe space, get into drugs or alcohol, or who are depressed, even suicidal even if not acted upon, do considerably worse in school.

For those that came long after I did, computers become surrogates. We spend most of our time, when not at school or sleeping, gaming, or interacting with others we have found like us. Parents will on occasion try to separate us from the computer but others, most others, will not notice at all because we are not causing problems and they have their own 'adult' issues.

I eventually found computers, but the PC was in the future, so I read. A lot. My parents encouraged me to read and often bought stacks of books for me. But it was my escape.

A fire happened in our house when I was about nine or so that made me very afraid of fire in any form and kept me away from smoking anything. This set me apart from the kids that would have introduced me to alcohol and drugs. And as most of the countercultures of the sixties and seventies revolved in some way around alcohol or drugs, it kept me away from them also. I turned inward. Socially, educationally, and personally.

Our siblings, like our peers, find us hard to understand or just weird. They make their rejections known in many different ways but mostly just by isolating us. Their betrayal, as we feel it, leaves us alone. Other adults don't seem to make any effort to figure out what is wrong, and often excuse the behavior of others towards us. Another betrayal.

We have only ourselves. We live in our heads. We find some forms of escapism, in things like computers, or drugs. We just survive another day. But the worst is coming, and the inevitable happens. We see it happening to others around us and if we understand it, or have been taught it, we search ourselves daily in fear.

And, before we have time to adapt, it begins.

Puberty.

PUBERTY AND THE TEEN YEARS
– GENERAL

The ultimate betrayal. Our own bodies begin to change, and the "serenity" of our earlier self-acceptance, such that it is, is shattered. We see what is happening to others and are horrified. While many around us are bragging and strutting their changes, we are dying inside. We begin to see the changes in our own bodies, and we have lost our escape, lost our one place of safety.

Puberty is hard on every kid. The changes, whether they are body, emotional, and/or social, make these years a challenge for all teens, parents, and other adults. But for us, the added issue of incongruity becomes a time of unbearable experiences; too much for many.

From a young woman of transsex experience:

I'm so tired of living with the trauma of my adolescent body developing according to testosterone-influenced changes, and no matter how well I pass or how well-adjusted I am, the memory of the pure, terrifying body horror of that time will never leave me. I have learned to be comfortable with my body, I have gotten surgery to make it match my brain's mental map of my body, but that only eliminates the dysphoria, not the trauma. The trauma is just going to continue to stick with me.

My mental image of myself has always been female. I don't remember any point in my life where that wasn't true, I just went along with the 'boy' thing because that's what I was told I was, and who was I to question my parents and teachers? And despite how frustrating that was to me as a child, it was something I managed because I didn't know there was an alternative. It was manageable, until puberty started. Even if I'm not built like a man, and I avoided quite

Every change brings more self-rejection. For the percentage whose body does not follow a common puberty timeline, the internal dialogue makes the knowledge the change is coming almost as unbearable as any change. And peers eventually notice any delay and that becomes another 'othering' item.

For the boy with incongruity, every change makes the likelihood of ever being accepted normally as a woman further out of reach. For the girl, every month of menses rams home her incongruity in often painful ways.

Teenage suicide is significant, and I believe, as do many others, incongruity plays a part in a significant number of cases. Teens that have a different sexual orientation have similar issues but often not the betrayal of their body.

Junior high and high school expose us to a much larger community that can give many more examples of how we live amongst the wrong group of peers. Away from parents, and only nominally supervised, we interact and tend to get exposed as 'other' all over again. It is about this time is when we finally get a name for our situation and nowadays, learn there are many of us.

People express ideas and behaviors that confuse us or are so outside of our experience that we usually fail to connect with peers exactly when significant social groups are forming.

Our dysphoria, previously, if only an intermittent thing, tends to get considerably worse during puberty. Every change pulls us further and further from our nature. We can no longer pretend; we **ARE** changing into something we can't even imagine having to accept. For many it is no longer just emotional or psychological, it is a physical pain. We go to bed each night dreading what the next day will bring.

*

Where things appear to have become murky today is the assertion that the experiences of incongruity pre-puberty are not universal. That there are supposedly individuals who have a congruent gender identity until puberty, or even well into adulthood. It is from my personal experience, and from talking with many others over the last forty years, that they fall into a different category. One that deals with many of, but not all of, the same issues and thoughts.

What is different between the two is that 'early onset' indicates that it is the true nature being expressed whereas 'late onset' seems to be in reaction to the environment. I am not saying late onset never occurs, but instead that it needs to be understood as a function of a teen's experiences.

I accept this but disagree with the assertion that they are the same as those of us who recognized of our incongruity early. That does not mean they shouldn't get care, or that they are not gender incongruent, just that they have a different foundation to their issues, and that needs to be considered more thoroughly when involved in therapy and decisions about surgery.

• Parents

Hi Mom and Dad,

I want to be a girl. I should have been born a girl; I AM a girl.

I want to be a boy. I should have been born a boy; I AM a boy.

Yeah, that is going to go over like a lead balloon. But what can we say? Most are more hesitant and figure a letter laying everything out would be better. I've heard of both positive and negative outcomes to that approach. What I can say is that for the most part, the dialogue in our head of what to say and who to say it to goes on for years!

Most, if not all, parents of gender incongruent children are confused. They don't understand where this is coming from. They had a happy baby, what changed? We learned we were different, and when it showed, it created upset and friction.

Fathers see sons becoming feminine (though we were all along) and, too often, it upsets them to the point that their punishments tend to go over the line. Call it shame, or fear, or guilt; whatever the reason they can't deal with their child's incongruity. They want their 'son' to grow up like them or their version of what a man should be.

Fathers often only see a divergence from their own expectations. Rather than seeking an understanding of their child, they reject them or worse, attempt to impose conformity at all costs. On the positive side, there are fathers who accept their child regardless of the perceived issues, but they are as rare and precious as any perfect gemstone.

Mothers appear better able to handle a 'son' who is feminine but her response to a 'daughter' who is masculine tends to mirror many of the same behaviors as the fathers' response to the opposite case. Mothers want their daughters to be like them – or to be better.

In talking with my own parents and the parents of others that I have known, mothers know something is wrong often before we are aware of it ourselves. How our nature falls into norms but the norms for the opposite sex. Or that we just don't seem happy. What causes distress for many of us is if only we had spoken of these concerns earlier in life, things may have gone differently.

My mother tried to get me to talk about myself (I had been caught in girl's clothes), but I refused. I believed that it wouldn't matter and would only cause more issues. Even looking back, having talked to my mother years later when I did transition, and now, 50 years later, I hold the same view. Not because I felt my mother couldn't deal with it, but because our society and culture could not.

Mothers have their own understanding of the world and how it tends to treat those who don't fit in differently. They do not want their child to face those torments. They don't want to identify something as the problem when they don't know if it's accurate or not. They are concerned, and rightly so in some cases, that they will be offering an explanation that only seems to fit rather than an actual understanding of what is wrong.

Whatever the reason, some parents rear back, seemingly in revulsion at their child's incongruity. Their strong reaction creates a sense of fear in the child that is so pervasive that there is no safe place to retreat to. We have vocal and physical bullying in school and in our neighborhood. And now it is no different at home. This situation puts a child into a never-ending fight or flight state with no respite from it anywhere or with anyone. It causes mental health issues that will persist for the life of the child. While the root issue is gender incongruity, dealing with that alone will not resolve the nightmares children have from their childhood and parents.

Parents that reject a child who is incongruent essentially demand that we deny ourselves to conform to their expectations. They are not looking at their child as a unique living, breathing, human being, but rather the personification of some ideal they have for their child. Is that a harsh accusation? Am I wrong? Could it possibly be that the parent wants the child to grow up healthy and therefore they consider the current issue to be unhealthy? So rather than accepting it, they force their child away? I have heard many argue that their child has been damaged or corrupted by others, or by the internet, or by drugs. Anything to deny the possibility that their child could actually be gender incongruent.

I would like to say that parents that act so have demographic things in common, but that would be untrue. It seems that regardless of religion, politics, or economic status, too many parents put something else above the health and welfare of their child; be it social standing, religious devotion or just their own masculinity or femininity.

I will note that parental attitudes on this are trending better as more parents are at least somewhat better aware or at least somewhat informed about gender incongruity.

> *For my parents, shame played had a small part, but fear was the dominant factor. Fear for my physical wellbeing, and fear for my future happiness and success. My mother once asked if all the bullying when I was younger was because of my 'secret.' I told her no one knew it; but they did know I was different.*

Parents promote, encourage, or demand conformity to the status quo – that you are what you were born to be. In the last five to seven years at least in North America, Europe, and Australia, this has begun to change. Parents are more aware of gender incongruity and are more open to help their child who is dealing with incongruity. However, there is a negative to it also: some parents are equating gender non-conformity with gender incongruity. They are not the same nor should they be treated the same.

How does a parent know if their child is gender incongruent, rather than being gender non-conforming, or dealing with another issue? It goes back to understanding the behavior of their child from an early age. Was there non-conforming behavior early? Parents need to try to be objective in their recollections. But further, they need to understand what is going on in their child's life. Too many parents are not aware of the bullying, educational difficulties, and social anxieties.

We don't appear out of nowhere. In cases where teens, or those just entering puberty, bring up gender incongruity, it is up to the parent to understand the issues surrounding their child's statements, as well as what gender incongruity is and means. Don't dismiss, but don't blindly accept either. Getting an experienced therapist involved is necessary (but be aware of the issues surrounding therapists recently – see here),

I want to encourage parents to be persistent, tender, open, and talk with their children. Not just the incongruent ones. Any child that finds him or herself to be different needs support at home. But incongruent children can cause parents to feel blame for the situation.

YOU ARE NOT TO BLAME.

Neither are we. But as noted earlier, it only takes a single instance of disdain, or of rejecting the concept of 'wanting to be the other'; No matter how innocent or minimal the parent thinks it is, that is enough for us to bury the idea of ever talking about our incongruity with you. Understand, when we are young, we often take everything literally. We don't understand nuances, or implicit exceptions. We see every rejection of 'other' as a reflection of your rejection of us. Again, I am not blaming you, unless you are aware of our incongruity, your actions are not directed at us.

But if you do know, and reject the idea for your child, it will probably destroy the relationship and leave your child damaged for life.

– YEAR ELEVEN AND TWELVE

For incongruent 'boys', the change is basically an emotional death sentence. Every hair that sprouts will likely need to eventually be permanently removed. Every inch of height forever changes perspective. And when the voice begins to deepen, it becomes very difficult to raise it again. Bone structure hardens the fundamental shape that increasing muscle mass defines.

Where peers cheer every change, we often cry alone. The incongruent girls are seldom any better off, but they will soon face a step that literally wracks their body every month. Their pain isn't just psychological or emotional, but actually physical. Menses' is a monthly reminder not only of their body's betrayal, but mothers and other women seem to be almost gleeful that their sometimes too masculine daughter is actually becoming more feminine. And if menses weren't enough, breast development is very difficult to hide or ignore.

Every little change makes our hopes, often held for years, of being acceptable in other's eyes less and less likely. The incongruent 'boy' that grows to 6'3" and 220 pounds, rightly worries about ever appearing feminine.

The incongruent 'girl' who stops growing at 5'1" and 115 pounds knows other men will never let her forget her stature, and those breasts will need to be come off in a way that can scar her forever.

A note on pronouns: Current convention is that when someone identifies as gender incongruent, we use the pronouns associated with their gender identity not their physical sex. I am not doing so because at this time in the life of our gender incongruent children/teens, no one knows (except maybe some people they have found on social media). Even our internal dialogue often reflects the current biological and physical reality, rather than our own sense of self.

Our internal dialogue initially reflects our environment growing up. Everyone called us boys or girls. Our name was our name – we never knew there could be an alternative. But at some point, we recognize that the only place we could be truly ourselves is in our head. We begin to mentally refer to ourselves using the terminology of the other sex, or our gender. And many of us decide on a correctly gendered name for ourself.

On occasion, the gender incongruent 'boys' will feel emotional but are pressured to suppress it. In the words of male teachers, coaches, and even fathers: "man up!" Many become withdrawn and socially isolated. The gender incongruent 'girls' however occasionally seem to be angry, strongly rebellious. Are these stereotypes? Yes, of course. Where do you think they come from?

It is also the time that kids begin to recognize others as 'love' interests. In this we tend to stand apart because even if we recognize it, our interests are very different. Also, a burgeoning sexual awareness can confuse the issues greatly. Yet we are subject to our physical body. We hate it when we recognize someone as good looking because our body reacts – using the very parts that cause us the most distress.

Incongruent 'boys' find they spend their time looking at girls not with relationship interest, but to learn. Incongruent 'girls' often find a more general acceptance with boys but often for different reasons than expected for them.

Adolescents with gender incongruity walk a minefield of sexual and social hazards. Tie those in with normal puberty issues and it's no wonder many end up on medications or self-medicating.

Too often parents and even medical professionals dismiss these teenage issues as being driven by puberty, rather than by gender incongruence. At least, if they are even aware of the possibility of such an issue. Teens, despite already beginning to assert some level of independence, are still very reluctant to express their incongruity in any way, despite the emotional and psychological pressures puberty is causing them. So, the stress accumulates.

These feelings and awareness of alienation from the physical/sexual group we were born into are magnified by the physical changes and the emotional changes us and our peers are undergoing. We are certain we are in the wrong sex category because of the numerous differences in how we perceive and respond to external events. Now, those differences are no longer just in our internal comparisons, but are on display over and over again in our daily lives.

Males tend to become more assertive, competitive, and overt in their approaches to the opposite sex. This is typical behavior, but it is not what the gender incongruent 'boy' considers appropriate for them.

We became othered for reasons our peer groups seldom could articulate, but we noticed the differences and held back during our elementary and middle school years. Now our peers are noticing clear differences in our actions, reactions and emotions and we are now excluded because, to our peer groups, we don't fit in. Teenage male peers see the differences in the mannerisms and attitudes of incongruent 'boys' and deride them as 'girly' and the abuses grow. On the other end, the incongruent 'girls' are often dismissed as butch lesbians because we are not 'girly' enough.

High school activities like sports, organizations, and peer grouping tend to isolate us. However, some desperate incongruent teens try to in, with some relative success. This makes parents and other adults less likely to be concerned about our previous missteps in hiding our nature.

> *I engaged in a sport, golf. I tried to fit in. I could act appropriately even if it felt off too often. I made some friends but near the end of my first year, bullying resumed from people I previously had little or no contact with. It made no sense to me other than they just didn't like me, for whatever reason.*

> *I joined Junior Achievement (JA) via an afterschool program and there, amongst what we would call the 'geek squad' I found peers that I related to better because in that environment, gender didn't matter. It balanced the alienation I felt in school.*

> *None of the people in the sport, nor JA, lived in my neighborhood, so except during those activities, I was often locked into my books and my own head.*

The emotional stewpot in the beginning of puberty makes the adults involved to be wary of kids behaving outside expectations. Some teachers are sensitive to the differences, and a few make a special effort to engage. But some are, if not indifferent, antagonistic to differences. We stand out. No matter how hard we try.

By the end of the first year of high school, ages late 13 to early 14, much of our future school experiences are set. And few will be able to overcome the negative ones.

Divergence

There are many changes happening in society today with regard to those who are gender incongruent. First, parents are more aware. Second, other adults, such as teachers, are more aware and on the lookout. Third, the medical community has not only become more aware, they have become more proactive in dealing with the incongruent. Generally, these are all good things. However, with every societal change, there are those that demand the status quo, fight against the change, and refuse to even attempt to understand the particulars.

General awareness has helped many of us get better medical treatment and gain support within families and peers. However, it is dangerous for a young teen, seeing the overall acceptance, to believe such acceptance will be forthcoming within their own lives. Many parents are among those seeking to maintain the status quo, fighting the change they really don't understand.

I will try to avoid getting into the politicized nightmare that is unfolding as I write this, but it is enough to know that forces are gaining strength to demand many of the advancements made over the decades to create a better quality of life for the gender incongruent are to be repealed or returned to the previous status quo.

What is the previous status quo? No medical treatment for minors except mental health therapy. Make people suffer until adulthood before any medical change is allowed.

Consider the following, which do you think is more painful:

> *A 13-year-old learning that it might be 10, 20 or even 30 years before some kind of treatment becomes available to help deal with their gender dysphoria; or*

> *A 13-year-old learning that there is medical help to deal with their dysphoria right now, but they can't have it until their puberty runs its full course.*

Of course, knowing there is a medical way to address your pain and having it withheld because of political interests would be devastating.

But the first situation was what I faced back in 1971. And the second is what kids are facing today. I think the second is intolerable.

There is an argument to be made that life altering medical procedures should not be undertaken upon minors without significant understanding by everyone involved, including the teen, to the extent possible. But what is significant understanding?

People are arguing that medical intervention to correct our 'birth defect' is premature. That we need to live with our issue, despite the ability of the medical community to address it, because there are people that cannot understand our situation (or don't want to) and they have the political ability to prevent the medical community from acting. That we need to suffer because people find our situation difficult to understand or outright reject the entire concept of gender incongruity.

Choices have consequences and life altering medical procedures can have very long consequences that few people, even adults, fully realize. But we realize them. We see them every day.

This being said, I understand that there are people who received treatment as minors and now regret their choices. They argue they should never have been 'allowed' this choice and that the adults around them are accountable for their current condition. They are called de-transitioners and have gained a significant voice.[23]

For a long time, I opposed medical intervention in the lives of minors with gender incongruity. I felt, because I had survived, that they would too. Unfortunately, I found that I was putting my own experience in place of theirs. Over the last five years I have changed my mind with regard to several issues. Specifically, I considered the pain of someone knowing there was a treatment available, and it was being withheld until most of the damage was done because of a political viewpoint.

Let me say, that looking back, if puberty blockers were available to me back in my teens in the 1970s, I would have jumped at the chance. I know how much puberty cost me, looking back. Remember that young woman we met earlier, and her trauma caused by dealing with the effects of the ;wrong' puberty. Her lament has been felt at some point by *every single* gender incongruent person.

---

[23] We will look at a UK Court case concerning this issue next.

Up until this point, what has been described in previous sections has been common to almost all of us born incongruent. From the mid-2010s onward, the later example above has become almost the norm in North American, Europe, and Australia. That is being challenged. There must be common ground, some sort of compromise that can be reached.

Essay: Treatment of Minors with Gender Dysphoria[24]

First, an article:

> *On Tuesday, Britain's High Court defended young children from the transgender movement's rush to give kids experimental drugs that put them on a path to chemical castration. The court laid out a framework for considering whether minors under age 18 might be able to give informed consent to receive experimental so-called "puberty-blocking" drugs intended to treat gender dysphoria (the persistent condition of identifying with a gender opposite one's biological sex).*
>
> *In a groundbreaking ruling that should set the standard for such complex issues, Dame Victoria Sharp concluded that puberty-blockers are experimental, that their effects are not "reversible" as transgender activists claim, and that in order to consent to receive such drastic treatment, children must understand adult concepts that are almost certainly beyond their grasp.*

Let me start off by pointing out something that is ignored in the above but explained later that puts a slightly different spin on things.

> *Sharp described the use of puberty-blockers for children going through puberty at the right age as "very unusual" because "there is real uncertainty over the short and long-term consequences of the treatment with very limited evidence as to its efficacy, or indeed quite what it is seeking to achieve."*

---

[24] The essay was written in 2021 following the results of a court case in the UK brought by an incongruent male that had transitioned, and then detransitioned blaming her doctors for pushing HRT and surgery when she was too young to understand the consequences.

Worse, "there is a lack of clarity over the purpose of the treatment." While GIDS[Gender Identity Development Service] has claimed that puberty-blockers give children a "pause to think" about gender identity before they proceed to irreversible cross-sex hormones, transgender advocates have also suggested that puberty-blockers "limit the effects of puberty, and thus the need for greater surgical and chemical intervention later" in cases where a child persists in his or her transgender identity.

Finally, "the consequences of the treatment are highly complex and potentially lifelong and life changing in the most fundamental way imaginable. The treatment goes to the heart of an individual's identity, and is thus, quite possibly, unique as a medical treatment."

The blockers do not, by themselves, cause permanent sterility. It is cross-sex hormones that do that. But the concern being raised in the article is that less than 2% of those that go onto puberty blockers come off them and resume their standard puberty. But, because of that low rate of rejection, puberty blockers are considered the first step in the process of reassignment and the consequence of that process is complex and far reaching.

I don't see a problem with puberty blockers, even for pre-pubescent kids[25]. My concern is that minors are not getting good support and advice from the adults around them. Parents are not evaluating the child's full history; they seek to respond to the societal pressures for resolution of issues with clear dimensions. And the medical community appears to be compromised, and as a result is failing to treat each child as a unique patient, opting instead for a one-size-fits-all assembly line approach to 'get'm in, get'm out'.

The details of the case are informative:

GIDS set Bell on a path to puberty-blockers at age 16 and she started taking testosterone at 17. By age 20, she realized "the vision I had as a teenager of becoming male was strictly a fantasy and that it was not possible. My biological make-up was still

---

[25] Blockers have been used for children undergoing what is called precocious puberty – one starting very early – for years. Their use is well understood and not experimental.

female, and it showed, no matter how much testosterone was in my system or how much I would go to the gym. … I felt like a fraud, and I began to feel more lost, isolated, and confused than I did when I was pre-transition."

Three things here: she had already entered puberty, within a year she was on cross-sex hormones, her expectations were unrealistic, and she had non-gender related unresolved issues not related to gender prior to transition.

Once she had begun menses and had breast development, only surgical intervention would have changed them. Testosterone would not of itself change them – though menses probably would have been interrupted. The time on blockers was relatively short – this is the time for consideration and determination of underlying issues. Her self-described 'fantastical' expectations should have been talked through with a therapist but apparently were not. The medical community accepting the conclusions of a teen alone as sufficient evidence of appropriateness is malpractice.

For the female incongruent teen, hormones have a strong impact that cannot be reversed even early in the process. Voice change and hair growth can start as soon as 60 days into treatment. For the male incongruent teen changes often take six months or more and are far more subtle and easily reversible. For that reason alone, the female incongruent teen needs to be better informed and be treated with much more caution than the male incongruent teen.

You cannot treat the female and the male incongruent teen the same medically. Timing, impact, the extent of puberty, and societal influences are different for both and must be addressed differently.

This bothers me greatly:

> *Bell claimed that she could not have consented to puberty-blockers at her age. Dame Sharp considered whether or not a 16-year-old child could be considered competent to consent to such an experimental "treatment" under the precedent of* Gillick v. West Norfolk and Wisbech Health Authority *(1986), in which the High Court ruled that minors could consent to receive contraception.*

This is saying: I felt the need to be able to control my body at 16 and then having regretted the decision have told everyone it's their fault for letting me have the control. My problem is less with the child than with the adults around them.

However, I also have a problem with this:

> *Yet the use of puberty-blockers to treat gender dysphoria is experimental. In such cases, "the consequences of the treatment are profound, the benefits unclear and the long-term consequences to a material degree unknown." In such cases, informed consent may be impossible, especially for children under age 16 who think of themselves as transgender.*

The use of puberty blockers in youth with gender dysphoria is not experimental. The effects are well-known. The consequences are profound, the benefits are clear, and the long-term consequences can be judged. But two things have to happen: the child must be evaluated objectively, free from societal pressures; the medical community must be assured that the full history of the child, free of prejudice, is considered and their current state of mind and expectations are rational.

It is also worth noting that successful cases are much less likely to make the news than unsuccessful ones, creating a skew in media representation of the issue.

Stopping puberty in a child with gender dysphoria is a blessing. The betrayal of the body when dealing with the issue of gender dysphoria has a profoundly negative impact on their self-worth and evaluation. If there are other mental health issues, they must be addressed prior to moving to cross-sex hormones. If they cannot, then changing sex is likely the wrong solution for an unrelated issue, to be an additional burden rather than helpful.

The following paragraph clearly fails to understand the nature of gender identity and the issue of gender dysphoria:

> *Even puberty-blockers do not make time stand still. They prevent a child from going through puberty in the normal process. At a minimum, this deprives him or her of "undergoing the physical and consequential psychological changes which would contribute to the understanding of a person's identity."*

A person's gender identity is established well before puberty. Other aspects of their personality continue to develop during, and after, puberty. But the physical and psychological changes of puberty can damage a child with gender dysphoria. Clear understanding by the parents and medical community caring for the child is needed – and right now, I have little confidence in either. And the court's order, and the article's author are insufficient to help fix it.

> *In order to achieve competence to consent to transgender treatment, children must understand eight factors, according to Sharp:*

> (i)   the immediate consequences of the treatment in physical and psychological terms;
> (ii)   the fact that the vast majority of patients taking PBs [puberty blockers] go on to CSH [cross sex hormones] and therefore that s/he is on a pathway to much greater medical interventions;
> (iii)   the relationship between taking CSH and subsequent surgery, with the implications of such surgery;
> (iv)   the fact that CSH may well lead to a loss of fertility;
> (v)   the impact of CSH on sexual function;
> (vi)   the impact that taking this step on this treatment pathway may have on future and life-long relationships;
> (vii)   the unknown physical consequences of taking PBs; and
> (viii) the fact that the evidence base for this treatment is as yet highly uncertain.

> *Children lack the ability to understand what fertility and sexual fulfillment will mean to them as adults. As Sharp wrote, "the meaning of sexual fulfilment, and what the implications of treatment may be for this in the future, will be impossible for many children to comprehend."*

To that, I'd argue adults lack the ability to clearly understand all the consequences if their mental health is compromised in any way. The demands of the Court show little understanding of gender dysphoria or the development of children with it.

The criteria of the Court, rightly expressed by the article's author, will result in few if any applications of puberty blockers to those under 16 or even 18. And I think that is a failure of the Court and of the effort to protect children.[26]

* * *

The important difference between kids at thirteen with gender incongruity and other kids at thirteen is that we have been dealing with our incongruity and its consequences for years at that point. We have tried to find information and understanding on our own (the internet age has certainly helped) and so we know what many of the issues are long before 'regular' kids ever have to begin to be aware of them. Like a child with a drunk parent, or a single parent, they grow up faster because there is no choice. We have faced aspects of our personality and nature long before others were often aware of them...

Is it realistic to expect that the majority of thirteen-year-olds are able to realize this?

Most of us know that we would have to give up having kids of our own. We know we would have to take hormones forever. And that surgery would be painful. All by thirteen. Did I understand the animosity, the violence, the weight of society against me? Nope. But I knew what my body had to go through to get where I needed to be. And nope, not all thirteen-year-old transsex kids do. They need good advice from objective, caring parents, and the medical community. That is not happening right now.

*

---

[26] In 2021, a court of appeals overturned the results of this UK case stating: "In its ruling today, the Court of Appeal said that it was "inappropriate" for the High Court to "provide the guidance" that trans youth couldn't consent to puberty blockers, adding that "the claim for judicial review should have been dismissed" outright.

"We recognise that the guidance stemmed from the understandable concern of the Divisional Court for the welfare of children suffering from gender dysphoria who, it is common ground, are deeply distressed and highly vulnerable," the Court of Appeal judges said.

"In our judgment, however, the court was not in a position to generalise about the capability of persons of different ages to understand what is necessary for them to be competent to consent to the administration of puberty blockers."

If there seems to be some inconsistency in my comments on the case and 'self-identification', let me try to clarify.

We spend years with doubts and uncertainty. But we are certain we are incongruent. We know what needs to happen to deal with our dysphoria. Now, we need to talk to our parents and therapists and allow them to gain some of that certainty. That will take time and patience on our part. Unfortunately, we are just reaching teenagerhood and patience is not our strong point. We cannot demand, though many of us do (at this age), that parents, therapists, community, and society accept our assertion at face value. For society to capitulate to those demands was irrational.

For decades the process was:

a)   identify as gender incongruent;
b)   find a therapist (psychiatrist or psychologist), hopefully with some experience in gender issues;
c)   engage in a period of therapy, usually one year;
d)   have the therapist recommend hormone therapy via an experienced endocrinologist;
e)   begin the real-life test (RLT) – a period of time living as the identified gender;
f)   continue therapy, usually for another year;
g)   get approval from the therapist, after a year or more of RLT, for surgery;
h)   find and pay for a surgeon to perform reassignment surgery.

I think we need to return to some semblance of the above – with the caveat that each person is an individual and needs to be treated as such. The process could take years, it did take years.

For me, it took five years. When I first heard there was surgery to fix my condition, in 1972, there were maybe three surgeons in the whole world that could, and would, perform the surgery and it cost a fortune. The number of experienced gender therapists in the world could be counted on one hand.

By the time I actually started RLT, sixteen years later, there were about a dozen surgeons and more than 30 or 40 therapists worldwide. In the United States, there were five

*gender clinics with therapists, endocrinologists, and
surgeons. Today (2023), there are more than 50 surgeons,
thousands of therapists in dozens of countries.*

One of the major changes in the last decade has been the abdication of the medical community with regard to the original standards of care for treating gender incongruent people.

By the mid-2010s, the process had been streamlined. Teens are getting approval for puberty blockers and even hormones with little therapist involvement, and surgical procedures are happening as early as fifteen. Rhetoric about 'gatekeepers' is used to skip the therapy that helps protect teens from acting without careful thought and screening. Yes, people lie to get access to blockers, hormones, and surgery. It is rare, but as fewer impediments exist, the need to lie becomes less – as long as you know what to say to the medical community. And the internet is a fount of information in that regard.

I want incongruent teens to get help. But at the same time, I want to ensure that it is the appropriate type of help and that requires time for therapists to get to know and understand the teen. Parents are being pushed and often dragged into agreeing to medical intervention when they don't fully understand the consequences. Or even the etiology of their child's situation.

As time goes on, the pressure we feel to tell someone what is going on increases. We feel alone and isolated and we need someone that can relate to us, preferably as who we wish we were. But how to find and tell such a person? Obviously, the best people to tell would be our parents but that is just fraught with dangers. And what would we tell them if we managed to work up the courage?

With the above in mind, I will continue with our experiences throughout puberty because even with the above in mind, most teens still deal with the same issues as those that came in the years and decades before them.

Essay : Trans Suicide, Not the Whole Story

The 2015 U.S. Transgender Survey (USTS), which is the largest survey of transgender people in the U.S. to date, found that 81.7 percent of respondents reported ever seriously thinking about suicide in their lifetimes, while 48.3 percent had done so in the past year. In regard to suicide attempts, 40.4 percent reported attempting suicide at some point in their lifetimes, and 7.3 percent reported attempting suicide in the past year.[27]

Over 80% of trans people consider suicide at some point in their lives. There are many reasons offered to researchers, but I think two are telling:

1. Rejection from family, friends, and community. Physical and emotional rejection leaves us adrift and without any support.
2. Bullying and harassment from peers. Continuous verbal and physical altercations wear down a sense of self. The stress builds with no relief.

Many statistics about our community are taken out of context. It tends to be easier because often the study sizes are very small and often conflicting. Both sides of the argument tend to pay attention to the information that supports its argument. One common false statement is that post-Sex Reassignment Surgery patients commit suicide as often or more often than those that do not undergo surgery. They don't.

We observed no increase in suicide death risk over time and even a decrease in suicide death risk in trans women. However, the suicide risk in transgender people is higher than in the general population and seems to occur during every stage of transitioning[28,]

---

[27] Suicide Thoughts and Attempts Amongst Transgender Adults:
https://escholarship.org/content/qt1812g3hm/qt1812g3hm.pdf

And

> *Prior to initiating unspecified gender-affirming treatment(s), 73.3% of the sample reported a history of suicidal ideation; this percentage dropped to 43.4% following the initiation of gender-affirming treatment. Prior to treatment initiation, 35.8% of the sample reported a history of suicide attempt(s), and 9.4% reported a history of suicide attempt(s) after initiation of gender-affirming treatment.* [29]

* * *

What follows does not apply to all of us. But much of it does. Many will demand proof, evidence that my statements are supported versus the 'studies' that prove far less than they think they do.

- When a child first starts to exhibit behaviors inconsistent with gender expectations at around 3-4, parents will either laugh about them, or, more usually, attempt to steer the child into behaviors more consistent with their expectations of gender conformity.

- By the time the child enters school years, persistent non-conforming gender behavior will usually cause parents to make stronger efforts that can lead to punishment for the non-conforming behaviors. By the time the child is 6-8, the child will recognize that those actions result in punishment and respond by either hiding the behaviors or pushing back against the efforts at conformity. Most children hide, knowing that their behaviors have caused a rift between them and their parents even if their understanding of why is limited. Shame, fear, and alienation become daily emotions

---

[28] Trends in suicide death risk in transgender people: results from the Amsterdam Cohort of Gender Dysphoria study (1972–2017)
https://www.ncbi.nlm.nih.gov/pmc/articles/PMC7317390/

[29] Suicide-Related Outcomes Following Gender-Affirming Treatment: A Review
https://www.cureus.com/articles/145464-suicide-related-outcomes-following-gender-affirming-treatment-a-review#!/

that in almost all cases will lead to various degrees of
depression as the cycle repeats.

- At school, and in the community, gender non-conforming
  behaviors provoke alienation from their peers and bullying.
  When bullying occurs, other adults often will turn a blind eye
  or sometimes will encourage attempts to force conformity.
  The bullying and lack of adult prevention of it creates an
  ineffective educational environment.

- By the age of 9 or 10, elicit activities that allow the non-
  conforming behavior, either implicitly or explicitly, reinforce
  the isolation. Fear, shame, and alienation grow to dominate
  their emotional state. Drugs and alcohol are often sought
  out, worsening the already damaging emotional
  environment. Depression becomes a foundation for other
  problems. At home punishments escalate and at school and
  in the community, bullying worsens.

- By around the age of 10-11 for girls, and 11-12 for boys, the
  only place the child can be ok is in their own self, but that is
  about to change: puberty is coming. At this point, the fear
  and yes, anger at the world, their parents, themselves
  reaches a point where there is little hope.

Maybe self-harm has already started, but if not, it often starts
here along with suicidal ideation. Parents either try to hide the
issues or seek religious or medical intervention to further the
punishment cycle rather than address the underlying issue. Their
own efforts to hide increase their emotional opposition to the
non-conforming behavior.

- The hormonal mix of puberty adds to the negative emotional
  state of the child. As they enter (junior) high school, non-
  conforming behavior brings increased bullying and tacit
  support of the bullying from other adults. Loss of support
  and betrayal from peers, outside adults, family members and
  ultimately their own body overwhelms the child. Suicidal
  ideation moves to planning.

About teachers and other adults and bullying: Often the phrases, "grow up", "get a thicker skin", "defend yourself", and "well, you were provoking them" are not supportive to the child or preventative towards bullying. Children see these adults as bully enablers and supporters.

Suicides at this time are rarely attributed to gender non-conformity issues. If suicide occurs now, there is little desire by parents or other adults to expose the reasoning, if known, for the suicide. A troubled child is often the only explanation offered to others.

- The teen sees three possible outcomes: nothing changes; suicide or repeated attempts increasing already significant issues; or attempts at conformity. The last will usually persuade parents and adults that 'it was just a phase'. The attempts at conformity occur because the body's betrayal is seen as inevitable. You can't fight yourself.

- Depending on the person and their attempts and relative successes, this period can last years and decades. For those that stagnate emotionally, their successes will be few. Those that attempted suicide might continue self-harming behaviors until succeeding in ending their 'pain' with few outside their immediate lives knowing why.

- Various levels of successful conformity are seldom sufficient to deal with the continued internal dialogue that often includes 'imposter syndrome' or shame at non-conforming thoughts. Societal pressures to conform causes non-conforming behavior in secret, increasing fear, shame, and alienation. Drugs and alcohol are often abused to varying degrees. Marriages fail and job stability suffers.

Suicides now are often unexplained or related to divorce, job loss, or drug/alcohol abuse.

- At some point, those that survive or get past the suicide choice, the non-conforming behavior becomes self-affirming behaviors despite the family and community demands. Family and job demands complicate matters, but the adult has at least the minimal ability to hold off those demands to initialize a self-conforming life.

- Societal pressure continues to perpetuate types of bullying. Peers and even strangers demand conformity, emotionally, verbally and on occasion, physically.

- **Stresses caused by hormone replacement therapy often mimic the emotional state of puberty all over again.** Suicide is not uncommon as the stresses build. Attempts by the adult, or others, to have medical or religious intervention, almost always to support the pressure to abandon non-conforming behaviors, add to the stress/pressure.

When suicide happens here, the non-conforming behavior is often the factor offered by others. The blame is put on hormones or transition itself, rather than the stresses family and community put on individuals that engage in 'non-conforming behavior'.

- People seeking to change sex (for themselves their gender has always been without question) post puberty deal not only with the pressures and stresses of their choice, but the consequences puberty dealt them – bodies that are difficult to 'pass off' as consistent with the presentation effort. The worse the situation (masculine/feminine bone/muscle structures, height, and voice), the more societal pressures grow. Bullying doesn't just exist in schools. It happens to adults on public transportation, in stores and in jobs. Verbal and physical abuse are common.

- Even post-transition, these pressures can continue. Often the emotional difficulties that permeated the non-conforming childhood remain unresolved. Parental abuse during childhood carries over into adulthood. The loss of family connections, fear of the past becoming known, and the lack of emotional support are all unresolved by completing a transition. Therapy prior to surgery should address, but often cannot completely correct the issues.

It would be helpful to the discussion, but beyond anyone interested, to understand to what extent the ability to be passing[30] or not had in a suicide at this point. Too frequently the simple answer, that transition failed to fix the problem, is likely the wrong one. Studies which broadly say that transitioning doesn't help whatsoever rely on few cases, wherein this factor is known and far too many adults seek to shift the blame for their own bullying or emotional failures.

For us original non-conforming children, we can do far worse within ourselves than our parents or peers ever do. We want to be normal; we want to be conforming; we want to not live in fear and shame; we want the unconditional love of our parents and family so many tell us is ours if we could just conform. But usually, it's beyond us to stop what is going on within us. Our true nature can be suppressed, but only at great emotional cost. And that cost is too much for many. The fear almost never goes away. We recognize that our parents and family are suffering because of our behavior. We often believe that our punishments are justified – that we are the bad people. Overcoming those thoughts is the goal of therapy, but that is ultimately achieved by understanding that we must accept ourselves first.

It is a wonder that any of us survive childhood and adulthood transitions. It is the external pressures that tip the balance. Always. And those pressures may never go away, even long after transition.

* * *

Whatever the reason, suicide is a surrender to the belief that whatever is happening today will continue to happen forever and there is no way to battle against it. It is a failure of every adult in a child's life. As I write this, there was a transwoman that was held up as a fine example of a successful transition that committed suicide, why we don't know. And just days later, a purported transman assaulted a school and killed children just after telling a friend he expected to die that day – what we call suicide by cop. How do we stop instances like this when we don't know what was

---

[30] Passing is the term for appearing in public, successfully, as our gender.

going on in their lives other than that it was clear they saw no value in living?

There is another side to discussions on suicide: this kind of statistic has been used by those that oppose treatment for gender incongruity. It has also been used by therapists against parents seeking to push back on their child's assertion of gender incongruity. And it has been used by teens to force therapists, parents, and the medical community to give them the treatment they demand, or else.[31]

WE, the community of incongruent people, need to push back against the use of statistics like the above for purposes of short-circuiting therapy and questioning adults. Many of us who have been around a long time welcome the increased access to medical transitioning, even for minors, but we have watched that access come at the expense of ensuring that everyone seeking it is adequately screened.

> *I never considered suicide. Certainly, never tried. For whatever reason, I got through bullying and puberty without thinking that I couldn't face a future.*

Teens today do not understand that society changes slowly, and the vast majority of people not only don't understand gender incongruity, they reject the concept out of hand. Nothing can force people to accept you, not even laws passed mandating it. We, they, have to learn to deal with the discrimination, deal with the abuse, and somehow still move forward with life.

➢ *Trauma*

There is one area that needs some discussion. Trauma induced gender dysphoria. Usually the trauma is abuse, often sexual abuse, which causes children/teens to reject their natal sex because they believe it was the reason for the abuse, or because they hope they will never be abused again if they change their sex.

---

[31] Suicide by Clinic-Referred Transgender Adolescents in the United Kingdom, https://www.ncbi.nlm.nih.gov/pmc/articles/PMC8888486/

It is vital that therapists understand these situations, and work to address the patients' trauma before considering any gender medical intervention. Over and over again I have heard harrowing accounts of abuse that occurred over the years. Extreme physical violence that if exposed would result in significant prison terms BUT because it was covered up (or dismissed) by the adults around the child, it never came to light. Worse, if that is possible, the violation of trust by other adults covering up the abuse damages a child's ability to successfully interact with others for the rest of their lives.

When the child or teen does not seek to remove the offensive genitals, they will often suppress the memories of events so deeply that it takes years of consistent therapy to recover them. And if someone changes their sex in the meantime, that can cause someone to reconsider years of transition and surgeries.

And like other forms of PTSD, it comes along with other significant issues. Drugs and alcohol only hide the problem under an avalanche of other interpersonal issues. Suicide is often considered, tried too often, and successful frequently. It's necessary for therapy to get to the root, deal with the trauma, and only then consider whether or not gender incongruity is a factor.

– YEAR THIRTEEN THROUGH SIXTEEN

By the second year of high school, dysphoria is beginning to overwhelm even the most stable of incongruent teens. Puberty changes continue to worsen and the hormone stewpot amongst the peers is in full boil.

Male peers are forming competitive groups and establishing their societal hierarchies. Female peers are building their social groups, and both are beginning the relationship dances that dominate the next five to seven years. The incongruent teen is being ostracized, at best, from their peer groups. Without support, and with little help from parents, the teen is alone.

There are two different paths these teens often follow: either engaging in alcohol or drug self-medication or avoiding it altogether. For those on the self-med route, school becomes just a period of time to tolerate their existence. For those on the alternative, school is a period of time to survive. If they can build even a small social group, they can be at least slightly productive towards building their future. These two paths diverge over the years significantly.

Too many on the self-med path succumb to overdose and other medically related outcomes making any hope of treating their dysphoria a rapidly retreating hope. They often have severe depression, which often will eventually lead them in only one direction. Far more often than we believe anyone is aware of. This is not to say that the non-self-med group has no issues. They simply don't complicate matters in the same way.

Strangely, the middle years of high school can establish some kind of stability that echoes back to those years prior to puberty. It may be a false sense of stability, but there is a daily sense of sameness.

The bullying often takes on a more serious turn physically for the male incongruent teen. Aggressive males seem to take a great offense to the idea of incongruent 'males', and physical attacks are common alongside the same verbal attacks that have persisted for years. While the incongruent 'female' is typically saved from the physical attacks, verbal attacks from females' border, and can often cross over into, assault. Teachers and administrators are powerless to stop all but the most egregious of acts upon both. Either they excuse, or ignore, the 'minor' infractions, or claim to be against bullying but shrug their shoulders saying, "What can you do? Kids will be kids."

Each of the groups, the congruent and incongruent, the males and the females, have entered into the period of intense emotional relationship-oriented behavior. The incongruent are on the outside of social groups, and individually are faced with society expecting them to seek the affections of the opposite sex while wishing and praying they could BE them. Even if they understood their sexual orientation, their current sex creates problems for them.

> *"Among 115 Dutch participants, for example, 33% of trans women and 22% of trans men reported experiencing changes in their sexual attractions. This was true of 49% of trans masculine and 64% of trans feminine individuals in a 2015 study of 452 participants from Massachusetts, with the majority of these changes occurring after social transition. In another 2013 study of 507 U.S. trans men who've started transitioning (including hormones and/or surgery), 40% reported some shift in sexual attractions. Almost identical results were found in a 2005 study of 232 U.S. trans women who had undergone surgical and hormonal transition, where 43% reported significant shifts in their sexual orientation (of 2+ points along the 7-point Kinsey scale)."* [32]

Trying to avoid relationship pitfalls isn't always easy because, for all the normal reasons, even incongruent teens feel the pull of relationships. It is the secret that causes additional complications. Many try 'normal' relationships in an effort to hide the secret behind the apparent normal behavior. Most teen relationships fail in due course. Though, the inherent nature of the incongruent can cause some partners confusion even if they appreciate some benefits from them.

As long as the relationships are not likely to be long term serious, males appreciate incongruent female's bias towards masculine behaviors

---

[32] https://www.them.us/story/sexual-attraction-after-transition

and females appreciate the incongruent males bias towards feminine behaviors.

Parents breathe a sigh of relief when their child engages in normal relationships; or they become more concerned when they don't engage in ANY relationships as would be expected.

It seems that most parents are just lost. They try to use their own experiences as teens as some type of guide on how to raise their own children, but the incongruent teen is way out of their understanding. If normal parents lack a context for their child's behavior, the parents of the incongruent teen can't even imagine a context.

As stated before, most caring parents fear for their child's future first and foremost. How to help them succeed is based on their understanding of how a normal teen builds upon a foundation of education and peer relationships in high school that helps propel them into college and beyond. But the incongruent teen has significant difficulties dealing with peers socially. While education success is more common than amongst the self-med incongruent groups, it often lags behind what had been expected by teachers and parents.

Parents again rely upon their own experiences, but they are of no real value in these situations. My own parent's experience was even further removed from my circumstances: they were immigrants to this country, were raised during the Depression and World War II, and went to religious schools.

For our high school teens, offers of involvement with 'professionals' to get help are like an invitation to the football team's celebration party – something to fear. And much harder to avoid. Today it is much easier to keep hidden and find like-minded teens online to commiserate with and with whom some support would be forthcoming.

With social media comes connection with others and information about gender issues and solutions. And also, additional avenues for bullying. Many parents have learned the hard way about the evils of social media and have been able to reduce some, but not much of the dangers of online bullying. Without supervision, even the nominal amount found in schools, online interactions can become all-encompassing nightmares from which there is little or no escape, even in the privacy of the teen's bedroom. Maybe especially in such a place.

Many teens now have grown up with computers and computer games. Parents loved getting kids out of underfoot and safely in the house away from the ever-growing risks in even good neighborhoods. What was an occasional diversion has become for most teens an obsession. Online social networks and gaming, often for significant numbers of hours during the evenings and weekends, has turned the bedroom into the teen's fortress of solitude.

As long as the teen is not getting into trouble and the school is not complaining, parents seem content to let the teen hide out. Attempts to engage with the teen seem half-hearted under normal conditions, and for the incongruent teen, out of touch.

For the incongruent teen, keeping their head down and out of trouble has become an artform. For the self-medicating incongruent teen, their slide from family and general society has been going on for years and is far too advanced for much chance of change without some significant event causing intervention.

In a few cases, in the right circumstances, there are incongruent teens that begin the process of transition. They inform parents and peers that they seek to change sex and want to at least begin the process of socially shifting from one sex to the other. Often caught surprised, a limited number of parents accept their child's desire and seek to help the process. More step up their previous efforts to enforce conformity to previous expectations. We will cover these situations more in a moment.

Getting through sophomore and junior years of high school, age 15 through 17, is an exercise in survival training. Learning to navigate the minefield of antagonistic teens, uncaring adults and the pitfalls of relationships is enough to keep even the best students dancing on hot coals.

But the last year brings further stress.

Transition: For the Teen

For decades, what we called the real-life test (RLT), happened well into adulthood. RLT while in school was impossible because we lacked the means. On the medical side, there were no puberty blockers and hormones were reserved for adults. There was no acceptance in the social arena and the culture was antagonistic at best, dangerous at worst.

This has changed in recent years, but many of the same issues that arise with adulthood RLT do still apply to teens. We don't want to make the medical transition process so onerous that no one can access care, even minors. But the process must be objective enough that those not appropriately suited for a medical transition get the therapy they need but are prevented from access to HRT and surgery.

What used to be called RLT, we call transition today. It recognizes that there is a process to get from one accepted sex to the other sex. It encompasses: the personal of parents, siblings, family, peers; the medical community of general physicians, therapists, endocrinologists, surgeons; the legal community of lawyers, judges, bureaucrats; and the rest of society of employers, landlords, the financial community. Each segment takes specific and concentrated effort to maneuver through.

We want to transition. The more we watch those of our gender (our opposite physical sex) living the lives we wish for ourselves, the greater the emotional and psychological pressures. But it requires exposure; it requires we talk about our core identity to people we want to trust, but who have given us reasons not to.

The parents and sibs.

Parents learn when their first child is two or so that many utterances said in the privacy of the home get parroted at the worst time in public. They forget that while those little ears may grow up, they never stop listening (teen years not withstanding)! When parents make derogatory comments about someone unusual seen on the street, or on TV, children remember and for the incongruent teen, they can't help but assume their parents will have the same type of opinion about them. Their sibs if they have them, will likewise listen, and take cues from parents. The result is an incongruent teen believing that if their parents and sibs found out about their secret, those derogatory comments would spur actual rejection, even physical rejection of them.

Being forced on to the streets because their parents reject them is a common fear. It happens, which gives some substance to their fear. Rightly or wrongly, that fear prevents us from even discussing our secret in any way or form with parents.

Yet, the social pressure to conform to expectations, of our parents, of our peers, of others continues to grow along with our own dysphoria regarding ongoing puberty. There is a limit to the amount of stress a person can take, and dysphoria is unrelenting. Our nature, carefully hidden, leaks like a sieve and those that pay attention often notice. It would be nice, and it does happen on occasion, that it is a good and helpful person, but too frequently, it is the wrong kind of notice.

At some point, it breaks, and the secret is exposed. The most common way? We get caught trying to alleviate the pressure by giving into the need to express ourselves as we wish we could. For the incongruent female, the risk is very low as "tomboy" is still acceptable. For the incongruent male, the consequence is nothing short of disaster.

We want our parents to know. We tried and failed to tell them. They were oblivious, or ignorant, about our nature and how it occasionally leaked out. But we need their support, their encouragement, their love. The risk we learned was just too high, yet our actions often were all but guaranteed to result in them catching us. It is the worst way for it to happen.

If, and it is a huge if, the parents are willing to at least talk, there is a chance for a positive outcome. It still might not happen. If there is shouting and name calling, the chances approach zero, and the potential range of negative outcomes grows to include those physical rejection fears. In either case, the cat is out of the bag.

It takes little or no time for the knowledge to spread to sibs and if parents are not careful, it gets free of the home in days. If the sibs are all smaller, so is the risk. And parents often have a strong desire to hold back exposure too. We are not the only ones that will have some explaining to do.

The conversation always starts with a variation on:

1. Explain yourself. What the hell were you doing?
2. Talk to us. We want to know why?
3. Are you gay?

No matter how many thousands of times we tried to prepare for this conversation, being put on the spot just adds too much pressure. The information we want our parents to have comes out in a jumbled mess. When it is just shouting and screaming, there is one thing that is clear, often the accusation: We are not going to have some pervert in our house.

<u>So, what is the information we want our parents to know?</u>

I love you and never wanted to hurt anyone. I don't know why I feel the way I do, but I do, and I have felt this way for a long time. Almost from the earliest memories. I would rather be NORMAL, but nothing seems to make these feelings go away. I have met a lot of others like me online. And no, they did not make me this way. I found them because I was already like this and I needed to know I wasn't alone, and I needed information about what I was going through.

I tried to tell you, maybe once or twice, but it seems that I really didn't know how to tell you. First, no one is to blame. There is nothing you did or didn't do. There is no one that did something to me, or hurt me, or forced me in any way. Dad/Mom, I really tried to be what you wanted for me, but I just couldn't figure out how. I kept hoping that I would turn out the way you wanted, that maybe things would change, just around the corner.

But nothing happened and I kept going to sleep, hoping, and praying that things could be different in the morning. As far as I know, no one else knows, but I think lots of people think I'm just weird.

What I was doing was trying to help the pain go away for just a little bit. If I could just be me, the real me, the person I want to be in front of everyone else, even if it was just for a few moments in private, maybe I could deal with things for another day.

I have accepted I am transsex. I was born with the wrong brain for the body I have. There are lots of studies and there is medical evidence for people like me, but whether they actually apply to me I have only my own feelings to go on. At some point, I have to transition, to begin the process to fix the incongruity between my brain and my body. And as I can't change my brain, it means changing my body to match. It is unbelievably terrifying for me, and I am sure you are shocked and confused but I have been dealing with this for years and you are just facing it now. I really need to know, what happens next from you?

The discussion can go on for hours, days, even weeks. My parents and I were still discussing things decades later. But as long as there is conversation, there is hope. Too often, parents are too upset to have a conversation then, even though they initiated it. They are not ready to hear anything we say. I often hope they will take time to first calm down. Second, get clear in their own head what they are feeling about what they just saw/found out. And finally, that they want to put their child's mental and physical wellbeing to the forefront.

I can tell you from experience, over the last thirty years and continuing on to today, the majority of parents don't do any of the above. Fear, shame, embarrassment, and anger are the emotions displayed often with devastating consequences to the family and their relationship with their child. In the majority of the cases, the relationship is ruptured for years. In way too many cases, permanently. It is not the health of their child that concerns them, but their standing in their own peer group and how others will, in their mind, treat their child.

I would like to tell you things have gotten better over the last thirty years, and marginally it is so. But regardless of demographic, too often parents reject their child out of hand, and permanently. It is not just the religious conservative parent; it is the openly supportive of the LGBT community liberal parent also. In these cases, relationships with siblings might survive, but often the parent's response dictates the sib's response.

The dysphoria remains and there is no longer any hope for support. The worst fear is realized, and the child is left adrift in a world they are barely prepared for.

IF things go even a little well, there will be a discussion about transition. What does it mean? When does it happen? As previously discussed, the old standards of care had a general process, even if not a hard timeline, of the steps necessary to effect a permanent change. And even if that previous process has been corrupted, it still offers the best guide to what to do next.

Certainly, continue to talk. Parents have a lot to catch up on and it is going to take time. We have been dealing with this for years, it is only right to give them a little time to come to grips with everything.

"Oh God, who do we have to tell?"

Family

It happens too often not to comment on but there is often one member of the family not surprised at all. It can be an older sib, a grandparent or aunt/uncle. Being a little removed from the situation, yet close enough for almost continuous contact, they are able to put those nature slips together and recognize something no one else did. Their sib, or grandchild, or niece/nephew isn't what everyone thinks.

Yet, there are lots of family members that will react negatively, just as parents feared. Even if the parent/child relationship survives, the parents' relationships with their parents and sibs might not.

Siblings have complicated relationships. Siblings of incongruent teens often take their lead from the parents, but much depends upon the existing relationship prior to the sibling finding out about the incongruency.

Consider the following situations:

1) A younger sibling finds out an older same sex sibling is incongruent.
2) An older sibling finds out the younger same sex sibling is incongruent.
3) A younger sibling finds out an older opposite sex sibling is incongruent.
4) An older sibling finds out the younger opposite sex sibling is incongruent.

When the same sex is involved, there is often a level of idealizing of the older by the younger. When the older sibling is incongruent, a younger sibling can feel a sense of betrayal. They have lost a role model, a mentor. When the younger sibling is incongruent, the older can feel like they have been cheated out of teaching the younger the ropes.

When female siblings find out their opposite sex sibling is incongruent, there is often a sense of privacy violation. A sense that the incongruent sibling is encroaching inappropriately.

In all cases, a sibling will worry they are going to be ostracized by their peers if they find out. Too often the result is a significant rejection of the incongruent sib. Again, it depends upon the pre-existing relationships. Sometimes siblings' bond closer because of the incongruency. Parents obviously have a significant influence in this potential outcome.

> *My sisters appeared to be quite supportive of my announcing I was incongruent (though I used the term transsexual at the time). My brothers were, at best, indifferent. But I found out shortly thereafter that the eldest*

I do need to note that while all my personal experience is in the United States and the UK - my parents were immigrants from Ireland and many of my extended family remain in the UK - the West is not the only place transsex people exist. In virtually all of the rest of the world, it is not just rejection that is feared, it is death. Many cultures do not accept the existence of transsex and will physically attack anyone that displays any such behavior or leanings. The percentage of parents and families that accept is probably **a quarter to half a percent.**

But the extended family is going to find out sooner or later, the better it happens from within the family. And from parents that have established some level of knowledge, even if not understanding, of their child's situation. Because every single question the parents have had, will be asked again.

Community.

Probably the hardest part of any transition is stepping out of the house for the first time in clothes that represent our gender. It is terrifying. Our fears are often overblown, but not always. There are places we will be ok to be in, public spaces like the mall or stores. Other places will be more difficult, school, church or at organized activities where we are well known.

How we handle are selves will have some impact on how we are treated. The more confident we are, the fewer difficulties we will have. Of course, we are not very confident at this point. But each time we have a positive reaction we will gain more confidence. There are two places where push back from others will occur with frequency and anger. Restrooms and school locker rooms.

It will not just be our peers that reject and attack us. Where the bullies only had their own animosity against us, now students we may not even have known, parents, and even teachers and administrators will join them on this specific issue. Very seldom do we have any defense, physically or vocally.

Still, we need access to facilities. There are options for compromise. Compromise that we feel is unwarranted given our efforts to get to this point, but they are necessary. There should not be blanket bans or assignments. Individual circumstances should be considered.

It is the incongruent male that provokes the greatest reaction. When transition begins at the beginning of puberty, we should be allowed to be integrated into our correct gender peer group. But once puberty has had some time to wreak havoc on us, we have to recognize there are things we have to acknowledge. For the incongruent male, puberty has, unfortunately, given us stronger physical characteristics: organ development and muscle groups. Just having different hormone levels does not remove many of those characteristics. Yes, muscle strength goes down for the incongruent male using female hormones but is usually still greater than that of natal females of the same age or stage of puberty.

Incongruent females seem to not have a problem gaining access; however, they also face significant issues once in those spaces if recognized. Natal males often think the presence of the incongruent female means acceptance of what happens to them. Physical attacks are common and often brutal. Administrators and adults turn a blind eye suggesting if they didn't want it to happen, they could stay out of those spaces.

Rejection is something we can often handle, even though it adds significantly to the stress of transition. It is the physical attacks and the betrayal of adults that are hard to accept. When parents are supportive, we have a safe harbor. When they are not, it seems as if the entire community has turned against us. People we've never met before attack without warning.

Transition during puberty can help prevent the kind of long-term trauma often associated with our resulting physical characteristics. Unfortunately, the emotional and psychological damage might be worse.

– YEAR SEVENTEEN AND EIGHTEEN

There are differences between the male and female brains. Research has shown that the incongruent male brain is more like a female brain, but not completely; the incongruent female brain is more like a male brain, but again, not completely.

There are structural differences that may suggest it is not just a hormonal imbalance during natal development that leads to transsex infants. Even if we come to understand the 'why' it happened, and even if the how is learned, WE still have to deal with the consequences for our lives. By our senior year, 17 going on 18, we know this is our life.

The damage done by puberty is not done yet, but enough has occurred that will make undoing it difficult, time consuming, and expensive IF at all possible. There are no procedures to reduce the male's height by several inches, any more than there are to increase the female's height by a similar amount.

Adulthood is just around the corner. We are faced with leaving the home we grew up in and facing a future we can barely determine. Our peers are making college and career plans while we are still trying to come to grips with our own bodies.

We need to consider WHAT our future can look like, and to WHOM that future will belong.

We were born with a body, and given a name, which has history. Do we apply to colleges as the person we were born as, or as the person we want to be? Do we apply for jobs knowing that we might not get to keep them when we transition? If we can't begin our transition prior to leaving high school, and the vast majority cannot, we have to carry our history baggage forward, gaining more weight as we go.

There is less need to dwell on the questions of why in hopes of an answer and more focus on dealing with our reality. But time has allowed for more knowledge. We have access to more information and at least enough education to read medical literature.

We have a name for condition: transsex.

We have a name for our suffering: dysphoria.

We might even have a different name for ourselves. Our parents might have had a name already picked out if we had been born correctly. Names of grandparents, or aunts and uncles, or other family members might resonate with us.

> *From about 12 or so, right up until I had the paperwork*
> *for my name change in front of me, I planned on being*
> *Katherine. I can't tell you why that is not my name*
> *now. I have no explanation.*

Where we get that name from varies, but we have started to refer to ourselves, at least in our head and maybe in online communities, by the name and the pronouns that are appropriate.

> Note: From this point on I will refer to the
> incongruent male as she, and the incongruent
> female as he.

We know we want to transition. Likely, family and peers will react negatively. So, if we can change our environment, such as moving away to work or go to school, we might be able to minimize their impact. Of course, that means sacrificing support mechanisms. Selecting a college away from home could allow us to begin anew.

Prior to the last decade or so, we had to move forward with the body, name and lives we grew up with. College, work, or for some of us, military service. Building on that history was, and still is for many, necessary. With more teens transitioning they have the opportunity to move on with their new lives unencumbered by their past.

Applying to schools means considering careers and life goals beyond just transitioning and surgery. But if we are unsure about how to, or when we will be able to, get on with our new life, what plans can be made? Parents and some teachers will often encourage us to plan lives we don't want. How do we deal with them and their expectations? Friends are looking forward to their futures and making their plans. They are often asking us what we are planning.

How to balance the competing demands? We don't have support or people that can help us mainly because we don't ask; we don't know who to trust.

There is another point of divergence here also: those that have self-medicated or not done even marginally ok in school, have a very different future. Work, to survive. Probably a place to stay that has a basic level of safety. Transition, at least socially, is maybe even more likely than for those heading off to college. And this is where a stereotype gets its substance. Many in this situation resort to sex work. It pays the bills and often provides access to hormones. I will return to them later.

If we have made it this far without disaster, it does not mean it is not just around the corner. Despite the somewhat lull of the last two years, the next year or two will fundamentally change our circumstances even without our dysphoria tripping us up.

Point 1) Some of us have begun to take little actions to adjust our behavior and appearance to advance our need to transition. While many changes provoke more of the antagonism of our peers, a few are ignored. She begins to grow her hair longer and take better care of her appearance. He tries to get away with hair cut short and more masculine type clothing. There are positive mental and emotional benefits to these minor changes, in spite of the peer (and sometimes parental) issues.

At the same time:

Point 2) Our bodies, functioning normally, have drives that 'normal' relationships can satisfy. Actively pursuing a relationship makes parents and others assume everything is ok. It seems to deny a desire to change.

If it seems that Point 1 and Point 2 are somewhat contradictory, then you might understand that while we acknowledge the depth of our need to fix our incongruency, we desperately want to be normal. We do things in private or just for ourselves that gives us some emotional relief, while doing things in public that hold up a pretense.

Maybe if we can just act normal long enough, the desire to change will fade; to fake it till we make it. Maybe the military will make a man of the incongruent male or allow the incongruent female to live in a male dominated environment. Even if we have accepted the reality that we are transsex, we continue to TRY to be normal. To act consistent with our birth sex and societal norms. We try everything people claim will help us get over the desire, the need, to transition.

We won't know until the damage is done, but nothing works. The dysphoria is always there, in the background.

To the parent, or friend that says, "You won't know until YOU'VE tried. Maybe it is different for you?" We aren't different. How can I make a blanket statement? Hundreds and hundreds of examples of people, including myself, trying so hard, so often, to **JUST BE NORMAL**. And failing. The dysphoria may fade into the background for a period of time, but it just doesn't go away. It is our nature. It is fundamental. And no matter how much our life might look normal, be normal, to everyone watching, our internal dialogue continues to assert, this is wrong.

For the few that can transition during high school, they will face backlash from certain directions, the religious, the phobic, the ignorant. But they will get through it, too often damaged by the effort of others rather than their own efforts. They will even find some acceptance, hopefully, most importantly, from within the family. And they will be able to focus on a future that does include surgery and the final changes necessary to live a full life, but also careers and family.

For the rest of us, we force ourselves to think of a future based on our biological status, to go with the flow instead of continuously fighting the current. We will need money and stability in the future if we have any chance. So, we apply to colleges, consider careers, and attend our final year of high school. A big enough change is coming to occupy us for the moment.

– GRADUATION

We finish school. Maybe we have a college all set. Maybe it is the military. But this final summer of childhood is for reflection and fear of the future. It is time for us to take full responsibility for our lives and the thoughts about what we face are terrifying.

Puberty has, for the most part, run its course. We have the body we will carry for the rest of our lives. For some, the result is nothing short of devastating. The hairy beast of a linebacker with the nature of a petite girl; the petite cheerleader with the nature of a defender. They know they will never be fully accepted for their nature with a body that belies it. For some of them they will play the part their body prepared them for, for decades and often, for the rest of their lives. It is not, ever, an admittance that their nature was actually congruent. Just a self-acknowledgement that the cost of transition is too high.

For most of us, we are in that range where with some effort, and hormones, we can successfully navigate society. But that is in the future. For now, we get on with the need to create a financial foundation, a degree or job, which will allow us, at some point, to transition.

We do a little reflection on our family, our peers, and the type of society we live in. We see where we started, how we coped, and what might remain in our corner as we embark upon adulthood. We are responsible for the future.

Returning to the point that what goes on in the US and the UK, and to a degree the rest of the EU, is not what goes on in the rest of the world. For those of us in those countries that do not recognize and who are deeply antagonistic towards the gender incongruent, we face a future of desolation. IF we can get out of those environments and flee to the US, or UK or Europe, we might have hope of a transition. But for almost all, there is nothing left to do but submit to the societal norms and live as we are expected to. And with the internet, watch as our peers change and transition and live their true lives. For too many, it is impossible. How many end themselves rather than face that future no one will ever know, but it is far more than many expect.

After this last summer of childhood freedom, we move forward alone.

ADULTHOOD

We are free to make our own decisions. Sort of. Our society has a say. But I recall one man's assertion on that say:

> Society can and does execute its own mandates: and if it issues wrong mandates instead of right, or any mandates at all in things with which it ought not to meddle, it practises a social tyranny more formidable than many kinds of political oppression, since, though not usually upheld by such extreme penalties, it leaves fewer means of escape, penetrating much more deeply into the details of life, and enslaving the soul itself. Protection, therefore, against the tyranny of the magistrate is not enough; there needs protection also against the tyranny of the prevailing opinion and feeling; against the tendency of society to impose, by other means than civil penalties, its own ideas and practices as rules of conduct on those who dissent from them; to fetter the development, and, if possible, prevent the formation, of any individuality not in harmony with its ways, and compel all characters to fashion themselves upon the model of its own.[33]

We are in a place where we need to conform to society's dictates in order to survive and obtain the resources we need to transition – a non-conformity that will cause significant disruption in our lives. How to balance our need to be true to ourself against the need to survive in society?

In a society that allows some existence at the margins, we can gain some of the experience we need. For societies that refuse to accept anything at or over the margins, the risks are potentially fatal. Being 'closeted' is a matter of survival.

So, how do we survive? Our dysphoria is managed somewhat by our ability to be ourself in private, but the longer that persists, the less beneficial it becomes. We want to live our life 24/7. We gather information and the materials needed to transition and plan. And plan. And plan. And the longer the delay, the more baggage of life we accrue.

---

[33] On Liberty, John Stuart Mill

The internet has given us thousands of examples of the incongruent stepping out and making their transitions, apparently successfully. We think of each example not as a motivation for our own transition, but rather an indictment of our failure to do so. It seems we take one step forward and two backwards.

Our work, and/or school environments demand a level of social interaction that we are immersed in, yet we hold ourselves apart from as much as possible. We get involved in relationships, general and superficial for the most part, but on occasion more intimate, which ratchets up our fear of exposure. Yet relationships do help with our emotional needs.

For the incongruent that attends college, many of the same issues faced in high school continue. Few can afford to live on their own and therefore share with other congruent students. In other words, the lack of privacy keeps us closeted. As college proceeds, dysphoria does build because as each year passes, life passes us by. We are stuck on a path we abhor but can't find a way off.

Another four years of waiting. Maybe more depending on our career choices. And for most of us, debt accumulates that will have to be repaid starting soon after completion of our degree. We will need to earn a living to survive and that living may come at the expense of the choice to transition.

Many still try to 'fake it' hoping that THIS year, we can wake up normal. That the need to transition will fade away.

– LIVING TWO LIVES

When we are teens, one of the ways we learn to survive is to, in the privacy of our rooms, we hide a few items of clothing and accessories that we can use to appear as our true selves. It is a risky behavior because we can get caught and most of us do. We end up purging the stuff and promising ourselves, and parents, "IT'LL NEVER HAPPEN AGAIN!" Until dysphoria and stress build again.

When we move out on our own, this process expands from a few items to two wardrobes, one masculine, one feminine. Obviously, each is used differently depending on which incongruent person we are. We keep this a closely guarded secret. Friends or relationship interests are kept away from seeing this private self. As much as it helps us deal with our dysphoria, it adds to the daily stresses.

Eventually, when we are comfortable with our private presentation, we want, even need, to venture out into the real world, as our real self. The fear of being seen appearing in one sex but being recognized as the other keeps us from doing it until the need becomes unbearable.

For the incongruent female, he has opportunities to appear more masculine even if puberty has left him with a body that is less androgynous that he would wish. His clothing choices, his hair style choices can be quite masculine and there will be considerably less blowback for doing so. People will just accept him, even if they can't quite be correct in their interpretation of his gender.

The incongruent male however has a much larger problem, and it is not just her physical appearance. If noticed, wearing the clothes that more accurately reflects her gender, she will get significant negative responses, not just from male society but many females will object also.

Unfortunately, neither, but most especially the incongruent male, will have had the opportunity to learn and make the mistakes of 'style' that teens learn through experimentation. Learning to appear and interact with general society is a function of teenagerhood. We never had that opportunity and no matter how closely we watched our peers in high school years, nothing is as useful as actual experience. So, we idealize what we wish we had been able to do. In the privacy of our own residences, some reach a level of fantasy that normal public appearances would moderate.

With careful efforts, we mitigate some of the risk and eventually begin to step out into public. We learn to be more comfortable in presenting our gender, and in interacting with others; generally, in our non-work hours and often far from where we live and work. We even try to be social, with limited success in some cases. Failures, people pointing us out and with physical altercations, tend to be too common.

If we stabilize our private life and our public life into some kind of balance, it may go on for many years. We remain single while those around us find relationships and marry. Eventually people recognize that our singlehood is persisting well beyond anyone else's. We generally make friends, often of the sex we long to be. Family gives up on their hope for us to find a long-term relationship.

But because of this balance, we hit a point where growth stops. We seem to stagnate at work and even our private time seems to be just repetitive rather than evolving.

But these two different lives cannot continue forever. One life will dominate. For many, the eventual conflict between them will force a transition. Timing is everything and, in some cases, it will be out of our hands.

We will be left a choice: continue bifurcated or give up whatever benefits and baggage our old life has and move forward. Some will be unable to choose, so choose neither and end the battle. Most will enter a formal transition despite the hardships. And a few will try to remain uncommitted. Till the next event

Something has to change, and the only real question becomes, are we ready? Can we face transition and the disruption it will cause in what has become quiet desperation?

.

– RELATIONSHIPS

Prior to transition, during transition or even post transition, we make friends. Maybe not many, but they are important to us because they exist in the face of all the rejection we face. Yet they are based on a falsehood that once exposed threatens even the strongest of bonds. We are not who our friends thought we were.

How to tell someone that has known us for a long time that we were born wrong, that we have a part of us that they never knew?

We develop a back story that is consistent with our current status that work with strangers or new acquaintances. But once those relationships develop further, we are left to either explain why we were less than forthright, or hope the issue never comes up. At some point, however, we become faced with situations where explaining our past needs to happen.

If friendships are fraught with stress, many engage in relationships to gain at least some compassion to keep the isolation at bay. Those relationships are based on a premise that in the end we can't maintain.

Most commonly the incongruent male will find herself in a relationship with another woman that is unaware of her true nature. These relationships can go on for years and often children are a result that complicates matters greatly.

How does an incongruent male engage in sexual intimacy? Fake it till you make it can demand a level of self-denial that has significant psychological complications. Anxiety, depression, and self-isolation all compromise the relationship and the incongruent male's mental health. Her wife, trying to understand, without knowing the root issue, has her own issues magnified.

The incongruent male wants children as it is in her nature to mother – but there IS a mother already in place.

Hiding, lying, becomes the anvil in which, eventually, the relationship will fail upon. The partner will believe, rightly, that the relationship was a lie from the start and feel very betrayed. It will be a weight added to the incongruent male's belief in their self-failures. On the rare occasion that the natal female will accept the incongruent male's nature, the relationship survives. But it is rare.

> *I did marry. I also made a conscious decision not to bring children into the relationship. It negatively affected our intimacy and while the marriage only lasted four years, it hurt my ex. I didn't intentionally set out to hurt her, but it was clear – years later – that I used her to try to be something I wasn't.*

It seems that the incongruent female enters into relationships less frequently – but the general acceptance of lesbian relationships may hide the situation. Obviously where homosexuality is abhorred and attacked, this situation can't exist either.

For both incongruent, the years pass. Work happens. Intimate and personal relationships are built and abandoned or fail. The dysphoria remains and a sense of losing time grows.

It is the incongruent male that usually has the long-term relationship that breaks catastrophically. In a repeat from her teen years, she is caught wearing clothes others consider inappropriate. The 'lie' has been exposed and those questions once asked by parents:

1. Explain yourself. What the hell were you doing?
2. Talk to me. I want to know why?
3. Are you gay?

Are now asked by a partner who often is devastated and cast adrift herself. Everything she thought she knew about her husband was false. If there are children, their protection becomes more important than the relationship because the wife's first thoughts are going to be about infidelity and homosexual lifestyles.

Few relationships can survive the situation and long before it's resolution, the incongruent male will often reach the conclusion the failure is for the best, it will release them to transition. It is a simplistic view that will be disabused all too soon. Spouses, hurt and feeling betrayed, will often explain to all that will listen that they were betrayed and their belief in the nature of the situation will often be very one-sided. She will not seek to understand. Families, friends and even employers will soon find out, in graphic and very incorrect terms, that the incongruent male is 'one of those perverts'.

Every fear, no longer held in the imagination, explodes into her life in very real, destructive ways. Transition now seems the only alternative, but it is being started at a very difficult emotional time. Not the best circumstances.

While the above is mostly from the incongruent male's perspective, the same situations often happen with the incongruent female. Children are seldom in the picture in his case, but the relationship's end will be no less destructive.

– WORK CHOICES

It is one thing to apply for a job as a high school student, quite another as an adult looking for full-time work. The college student has some flexibility if it is only a job for a paycheck. If it is meant to open doors for after college, then the question becomes as it is for the non-school adult, for who?

Thirty years ago, the idea of a transition in the same job was a non-starter. Even today, the complications are significant. It is much better to begin transition then look for a job. But even then, presentation and deportment matter. The first year of transition IS a transition period and trying to find work during it can be a challenge.

If you get a job after starting a transition, are you known to be in transition, or will the stress of being exposed be added? There are things you need to do before working in transition, foremost is identification then banking.

For those still pending transition, a job becomes a stricture on your plans. The longer you are in the job, the harder it becomes to leave. You gain a history in your field or industry that will be hard to avoid. And you can't just disappear – there becomes a gap in your work history you will need to explain.

You have a career. Financial stability. And leaving that for a transition can be daunting.

In the US, the UK and Europe, over the last decade or so, there has been some willingness by employers to work with incongruent employees, especially those with valuable skills and useful experience. They will help manage the workplace to ensure, if not a welcoming, safe environment. By transitioning at work, the incongruent keeps the income flowing when we need it most. But for all the well-publicized examples of acceptance, there are far more that will not tolerate a disruption. Regardless of the skills and abilities, companies will react in many of the same ways as parents and spouses – with revulsion and rejection.

Long before this, we have to make choices about what kind of work we want to do as adults. It affects our choices of education and even where to live. The more specialized the career, the more difficult disruption will be caused by a transition – but none of us think about that at the time. We take our interests and career desires and begin to build a life that does not take into account our need to transition. It is a parallel existence.

Do we carefully consider our choices? Not really. The 'being of two minds' that began during puberty is actually well defined at this point. We function in society in lives appropriate to our birth sex, while our private lives are in direct contradiction to it.

As I said, I joined the military, as do many incongruent males hoping, like I did, to 'make a man out of me'. It is a forlorn hope but at that point in our lives, we were still hoping for a change to come over us and the faking till we made it, finally won. It doesn't. But we are in the service for at least four years, and it stabilizes our adult lives. We gain skills and experience and for some, it becomes a career. One that all but guarantees no transition until far into the future. And one that almost always results in a long-term relationship with someone of the opposite sex.

For the incongruent males that skip the military, or college, work is often amongst the skilled trades. Stereotypical male careers that challenge her to 'fit in'. For those whose puberty did the most damage, substantial masculinization, it hides our nature behind a thick and tall façade. And it often leads to the decision never to transition. Relationships and families often follow.

For the incongruent female, attempts to fit into masculine arenas are generally, at least marginally, successful though with some significant belief about his sexual orientation. If puberty did not leave him significantly undersized, it will probably work. Those that find ourselves well into the 'petite' sizing, will generally not find ourselves in those masculine environments we desperately want.

The incongruent female will often gravitate to careers typically male. Work will be a challenge even for those of us who excelled at schooling and experience because the environment treats us as a token. It will be dual tracked: at work will be the male environment we seek, but it will hold us separate. Unlike the incongruent male, he will find relationships difficult to manage. Women will treat him as a friend rather than intimate relationship material.

However, transitioning for him will be somewhat easier as society will accept his behavior more readily. The lack of a long-term relationship keeps the complication level lower, and our public/private life barrier will be less developed. His career choices will dictate whether a 'transition in place' is possible.

Employment needs to be consistent but that requires a level of emotional and psychological stability that many of us have a hard time maintaining. Job hopping happens. Our incongruity often compromises work relationships as much as private ones. Maintaining stability comes with a price – our other life hope suffers. Depression and anxiety are common and alcohol use is often significant. Relationships can add a level of stability but at a cost.

For those that give up, assuming we will never transition, work becomes a place of respite. Devotion to it usually means a higher level of success. A double-edged sword as it gives us greater flexibility and freedom in our private life. There is always the dual life and us swinging back and forth across the line separating them. It is amongst this group that you find people who transition very late in life. And right now, because of the difference in numbers in the past amongst the incongruent males and females, those will most likely be the incongruent male.

Sex work is too common to ignore. A percentage, how much is certainly up for debate, of incongruent males will resort to sex work to obtain an income, but also to be treated, roughly, as their preferred gender. It comes with a nightmare amount of risk and problems. However, some make it work long enough to accomplish a transition medically. There are long lasting consequences from doing so and I don't think anyone would suggest it as a viable option. Physical abuse, drug use and interactions with police mean that even when a transition is complete and she wants to move away from sex work, her options might be limited.

I've known several women that took this path and none of them recommend it but are quick to note THEY had no options available to them. I won't, don't, criticize their choices. I couldn't make the same choice and fortunately didn't need to.

A last word for those of us who stay with one employer for a long period of time. The longer we stay, the more difficult any transition will become. We need stability at work to offset the instability of our private life's needs. It becomes a crutch we lean increasingly into and on. If our private life explodes (a marriage that fails because our spouse finds out) and impairs our work environment, we will find regaining some employment footing difficult. Years of experience will not be enough to keep us afloat. Employers will feel the disruption is not worth keeping us through the turmoil. Those that stand by us will do their best, but like the zero-tolerance bullying environment of schools, they won't be able to protect us from everything or everyone.

– WHY RECONSIDERED

Doubt. Every single person we meet that knows of our struggle doubts our statements that we are incongruent. Therapists should doubt. Doctors should doubt. Family and friends should doubt. And we should, and do, doubt. How can you not when EVERY SINGLE SHRED OF EVIDENCE points to the opposite of our assertion.

Yet many of us want to pretend there is no doubt. That we are certain that this is the right course for us. In the face of such unrelenting opposition from others, it might be the only thing that we can do. But we do have doubts. That is why we hesitate to begin transitioning. It is why we are afraid for our future. But these doubts, expressed to others, give them the certainty that they are correct and that we are wrong to think we are incongruent.

The science is settled, according to those not in science, that we were born male and female and that is the end of the discussion. For them. The physical reality is sufficient. And because, very often, we respect the speaker, and want to trust them in their assertion, we try to take in their statements and contradict our own thoughts with those assertions. Testing them against ourselves.

The religion of our family asserts claims that contradict our internal understanding of self and we desperately want to BELIEVE. Even though our prayers were never answered, maybe because we were asking for the wrong thing; we try to pray and ask for the 'wrongness' to be taken from us, for us to be the normal people we are expected, demanded, to be. We are devoted, prayerful, hopeful. We wake up each morning hopeful that today, we will be as expected – normal.

Every assertion, no matter the source, claiming that we are just delusional, mentally damaged, spiritually corrupt, just plain wrong is taken in and given serious consideration. We want something to help us. We need something to change because the alternative, transition, is going to be so hard, so disruptive, so life altering that anything that can get us off that path will be, IS, considered.

We need the push back from others. We have to gain some level of certainty that we are not delusional; that the path we are on is correct, for us. If that means giving into the doubts, not to change the path, but to face them and have some kind of objective argument to rebut them. Getting to the point of decision on transitioning requires that we have faced our doubts about the right course of action for us.

Part of the purpose of RLT is to determine if we can live as our gender. We need to be stable in our transition: work, school, friends, and socially. We need it to know we are doing the right thing. But therapists need it also to give them confidence to recommend HRT and surgery.

The choice for surgery is still in the future, but we know that it is on the path we are choosing. Does HRT help emotionally? Can we function in our gender in society? The first year gives ample opportunity for doubting our choices. The aggressive pushbacks we get from family, friends, and even general society (yes, even today in the West), all make us wonder if it is worth it.

Such is RLT. All the bullying we had to endure growing up was unbidden. Now, we choose to enter an arena knowing there would be pushback; there would be bullying; there would be rejection and even possibly, violence. Is there any reason to believe that doubts wouldn't creep in? They may not stay long, we might have quick and easy answers to the doubts, intellectually. But all the pushbacks have a cost. No matter how strong we might be mentally and emotionally it wears on us over time.

Decades ago, ok, still in many places, the incongruent male gets asked, "Why do you want to give up being a man?" As if giving up manhood is some incomprehensible step. Ah, because I am not a man. For the incongruent female, the same question gets asked generally in the context of childbirth. How can we give up those things' others find fundamental about their sex?

We still don't have an answer to why, but we have decided it doesn't really matter. I gave up, we give up, eventually. We face the FACT that we are who and what we were born as, gender incongruent. Our brain and our body do not match, and nothing has changed that reality. Is it worth all this? We have an answer. We have spent years unhappy and fighting our dysphoria. Why doesn't matter. How doesn't matter. We are incongruent and we have learned what it means we have to do.

Doubts notwithstanding.

TRANSITION

– THE FIRST YEAR

For the incongruent female, male bonding carries risks of physical altercations. He fortunately doesn't need to worry much about physical intimacy because he is less interesting to females than other males. Even in non-intimate situations, there is the potential for physical contact, and he needs to manage those situations carefully.

For the incongruent male, female socialization, desired for years, is startlingly intimate.

> *Probably the first thing I noticed about female socialization was the regular discussion of intimate and what I thought was very private situations. Women talk about periods and relationships in detail even with casual acquaintances. Having never experienced female social groups before, I was stunned and quickly had to acclimate. In other words, embellish my past with similar experiences such as my first period starting unexpectedly.*

I talk to other gender incongruent in Russia, Asia, the Middle East and even parts of the EU and they have no hope for themselves. They live vicariously through others, but it is clear it seldom helps and often makes them feel even worse.

Their societies do not accept the premise of gender incongruence; the medical community refuses to treat and in most cases outright dismisses the idea of gender incongruence. There are no hormones available, no therapists to talk to, no surgeons to help.

In a population of eight billion, if the .25% incongruent percentage is valid, there are some twenty million of us. Eighty percent or more live in places where transition is impossible. Almost sixteen million will live their lives without the chance to transition. (Un)Fortunately most will never know there was a way to treat their dysphoria.

But that leaves just over four million of us spread out in age and geography. There are those older than me that did and did not transition. By my surgery date in 1993 I estimate somewhere between eight and nine thousand had already undergone sex reassignment surgery (SRS) worldwide. The estimate now, in 2023, is that about 150,000 have had SRS worldwide.

Earlier, I suggested there are two people in transition for every person that has undergone SRS. And two people that wish they could be in transition for each that is. But it appears those numbers have changed over the decades. I believe those have doubled. And I can't explain why.

I do not think the current estimates published in studies is an accurate representation of our actual community size.[34] I don't think we can get any accurate numbers until we have a medical community acting objectively, patients answering honestly, and governments gathering statistics responsibly.

Regardless of the community size, each of us hits a point where the decision to transition cannot be put off any longer.

This was my point: I had divorced. I returned to my parents' home and returned to college (per their conditions on my return). I completed my first two years and was ready to move to a university to complete my degree. And I had been experimenting out in public as a woman. I was ready to begin my full-time transition but terrified. I considered the following questions and answers:

1. Was I, at some point, going to transition and get SRS? Yes.
2. Did I believe that having done so I would be happier? Yes.
3. Would, when I had done SRS, I have any regrets? Yes, that I waited as long as I did.
4. Then how could I justify waiting one more day?

Earlier I laid out the process of transitioning in the past and argued for a return to that process. For the incongruent adult, the process is more difficult because there is more past, to their past. I indicated four groups of people that someone has to engage in to complete a transition:

---

[34] A study published in 2022 suggested that as many as 11% of the teen population identified as transgender.

- Family
- Medical community
- Legal community
- Financial community (which includes workplace)

Family is still part of the process to the extent they have to be told, and told they will be, eventually. Obviously, the medical community needs to be engaged but without parental involvement at this point. The incongruent adult also has greater freedom of movement to travel and choose where and to whom they select for medical care. Social transitioning prior to any of the above does happen but usually, the first step is engaging the legal community.

We need to legally change our name. In most accepting countries the process is fairly straightforward. Submit the paperwork, wait the appropriate amount of time, and it is done. The process of dealing with all the places our name is used to define who we are is often, but not always as straightforward.

Changing our name divides our life into the past as the person named by our parents, and the future with the name we have chosen. The name represents, even if not directly by its etiology, our self as we have always seen ourselves. This is who we should have been from the beginning. Our true self, our correct self.

Within the community, the past name is referred to as our deadname. For some it means to kill the past and forget it. I think it means that we are born anew, with a new chance of living as we should have. People referring to us with our original name are, whether they understand it, or accept it, or not, refusing to acknowledge that we ARE changed, changing. It is a demand that we revert to the status quo, that we deny ourselves to conform to their expectations. For apparent reasons, we reject that demand. We can't stop people from using our past name, but we can, and do, limit opportunities for them to engage with us. Which usually means restricting our interactions with family and past friends.

Most of us, in the future, will guard the exposure of our birth names. It is the past.

Government entities such as social services need notification. Documentation might allow the name change, but if sex is noted, those entities might require surgical confirmation before allowing that designator to be changed. Still, with the identification corrected. We can begin to create a history with our true/real/new name. Up to here, we can begin the transition process without lots of drama in our day-to-day life but that is about to change.

Housing is next. In many cases it is a non-issue except for neighbors that may have met and known us in a pre-transition state. Now, faced with our transition, some will object. As long as it is not our landlord. Some landlords will take the side of neighbors that our new presentation is disruptive (or worse) and demand we relocate. Many places in the West have regulations to prevent such, but while you fight legally, you still need a place to live.

The first part of the financial community, our financial assets, is next. Bank accounts, debts and access methods all need addressing. Some can be done in less than an hour, others will take months. But we need your financial house organized because the next step will require it.

Work.

Letting a company know we are going to be transitioning will be a nightmare scenario. The larger the company we work for, the more likely the nightmare will be more in our mind, than in reality. But small companies are highly dependent upon their customer base AND our involvement in it. If we do not have a customer facing position, the likelihood is that they will accept our transition with some grace. If their customer base is conservative (not in the political meaning of the term), and our position is customer facing, the likelihood is that they will not accept our transition and give us the ultimatum: forget the transition or leave. Too many just fire us on the spot. Sure, in many places in the West you can sue them, but that means MORE exposure and greater risk.

And that is a consideration we have to make BEFORE all of the rest. If we don't have a job, we don't have the means to support ourself. If we don't have those means, transition is DOA. We already know that we lack (usually) a support group to fall back on. This is a choice we own individually, and the consequences are ours alone.

Some companies are openly accepting and if they are an option for employment, many gravitate in their direction. Most of the time we are going to be the test subject for any acceptance or rejections.

The issues we face, with family, landlords, banks, and employers are difficult before we consider how we are reacted to in the public sphere. We need to have a firm foundation, mentally (and physically), in order to face the challenges. Yet, most of us deal with anxiety, depression, and too often drug/alcohol abuse issues. Yes, most of these can be addressed if we can get a handle on our dysphoria (the root of most of the problems). But this needs to be addressed responsibly by therapists. They have to be aware of the dysphoria and the roots of how it created the issues that gave way to all the situations earlier in our lives that provoked the mental health issues. Absent that understanding, therapists and doctors are treating symptoms. Uselessly.

➢ *Hell Year*

The first year of transition is hell. Pure hell. Allowing ourselves to be in public for the first time in our lives is beneficial, but the reality is far from the hope or expectations. We lack a sense of style in our appearance choices; our deportment is fragmented at best, non-existent at worst leading to all kinds of confrontations while out; we are nervous and people read that as worrying or threatening; we are unsure of ourselves and it creates hesitations and lack of decisiveness; no matter how prepared, we lack the wardrobe for 24/7 living though for the incongruent female, this is less of an issue than for the incongruent male.

> *When I started my transition in 1987, I could be arrested for appearing in public in women's clothes. I could be arrested for using the women's restroom even though I would be taking my own life into my hands to use the men's. If I was attacked, my attackers would be free, but I would likely be facing criminal charges.*

Nothing can prepare you for the hate and vitriol that will come your way. People you don't know, never met before, attacking you physically or 'just' vocally frightens you in ways you can't imagine.

Strangers reject the concept of gender incongruity out of hand. Regardless of the science, or medical support, no matter how we look, they will tell us to our face we are a perverted, delusional male/female, seeking some sexual fetish gratification. And they will be offended at our very existence. And very often they will say it loud enough that everyone within 100 feet will hear about it. They will seek to gain support from others that have never met you, know nothing but what is being spewed against you.

There is no defense. Attempting to do so will escalate the situation. At best you will be allowed to leave, too often they will follow you continuing to harass. On occasion, the police will be called, and we will be the ones in trouble.

In my first year I was attacked, several times physically, vocally probably more than a dozen times. The police were summoned on two occasions that I used public restrooms. Both resulted in understanding officers thankfully.

On several occasions I got home and curled up on my bed and cried uncontrollably. And I lacked the issues with anxiety and depression common amongst us. Going back out again the next day was hard.

The arguments for keeping transsex people out of bathrooms has been going on for some time. Interestingly, it is only the incongruent male that is the focus of the discussion. Apparently, no one seems to have a problem with an incongruent female in male bathrooms or locker rooms.

For the incongruent transitioning, there is a requirement from the medical community that we live 24/7 in our gender. That means in all places, at all times. What are we supposed to do when we need a restroom? Of course, people want us to not exist at all, but that is not realistic.

People have been murdered, brutally beaten, and their attackers claim they were defrauded and within their rights – and won. Sure, "good" people will condone the violence, in the same sentence they will say 'they were asking for it.' Transition isn't just about us trying to live our lives, it is about negotiating societies that seem bent on beating us back into conformity.

If the attacks from people you don't know frighten you, the attacks from people you do know will leave you scared to death. These are people you call friends, family. They physically hit you, slap, punches, things thrown at you. They scream profanities, call you every evil thing imaginable. For the most part, we just take it. We can't fight back, even if we know how. They are unwilling to listen, to even consider what we might have to say. Those that give you the chance to say anything will dismiss it out of hand.

> "I've been this way all my life."
> "Bullshit. I've known you forever and you were never this perverted shit."

> "This is a medical condition that…."
> "That's crap. Your head is screwed up. You need therapy, not transition."

We try to be rational, but let's be honest, this condition appears to everyone else to be completely irrational. Everyone can see, and many have, our physical sex and for us to say it is wrong just reeks of delusion.

If you have gotten this far, you might be willing to listen to someone you know tell you they are gender incongruent and might even be willing to consider it. But getting people to this point can take years of effort. For someone that has never been presented with someone they know, to suddenly be confronted with a friend or family member telling them they are gender incongruent, rational responses are the furthest from their minds.

It took years for my family to come to accept me. For many it never happens. The loss of friendships is universal. Sure, some might stay but, without malice, they will say things over several years that indicate they have not accepted what is happening but seem to be hoping it will all be some 'phase' you are going through, and they want to be there when it ends.

Parents are confused at best, angry as hell at worst. Nothing you can say seems to make any difference. Every conversation devolves into screaming and yelling. Siblings, following our parents, reject and refuse to even talk.

> *I started at university and kept my head down as much as possible that first semester. I eventually got a part-time job on campus and another off campus both with my new name and female presentation. Starting back in 1987, mine was a*

Despite the fact there are hundreds of therapists in the United States today, there are long waiting lists and few options. In the UK the waiting lists are years long. And the number of therapists with good and relevant experience is far fewer than most think.

My first therapist rejected me as a possible candidate for SRS because I lacked homosexual relationships. It would take me more than a year to find another therapist. Other therapists today have similar strange criteria for who constitutes a good candidate or not. Or no criteria at all except the desire to transition medically.

I've heard of therapists that reject us because we have a history of crossdressing, or no history of crossdressing. They reject us because we have a history of sexual relationships with members of the opposite (to our birth) sex, or a history of sexual relationships with members of the same sex. Or both. We can find therapists in the same community with contradictory requirements; there doesn't seem to be any consistency with regard to age, sex or experience.

Antagonism vs lack of support. A person that turns their back on us refuses to accept or support our transition, as much as we hate the loss, it is better that they leave. If possible, we don't close the door to them, after all they could come back accepting. But we don't need confrontations, which is the antagonism part. Many families refuse to support our transitions but are not openly antagonistic – working to hamper our attempts or actively trying to interfere. In my experience it is about 80/20, antagonist/lack of support. Although in the US and UK, that ratio seems to be moderating some over the last 5-7 years.

Every interaction with authority, government, legal, or medical, is another emotional effort we have to get through. Another invasion, however necessary, of our private life. Every interaction with a new person socially is a question as to whether we should discuss our past. The former is not a choice, but the latter IS. And our community is strongly divided on the issue.

Being 'out' and proud of our choice to transition works for some people. I think it works for them because in their specific environment it is safe to do so. Many teens and young adults see the current culture as accepting and think therefore THEY will be accepted. They see people on social media being celebrated and encouraged and think they can expect the same. In most cases they are very wrong.

Communities and neighborhoods can be quite insular and very UNaccepting. Even dangerous. As adults, we need to understand where we are within the communities we live in, and their nature and level of acceptance. Regardless of what the larger society or culture accepts, we need to be cautious. Those 'out and proud' examples are by far the exceptions.

Exposing our past to general acquaintances is almost never a good idea from a safety, physical and emotional, point of view. Should we discuss our pass with potential intimate partners? A vocal minority says we are obligated to. And a large part of the general society agrees.

Don't. That is my suggestion. If a relationship has the hallmarks of a potential long term one, then yes, we need to. Of course, the fact that we do so after the start of the relationship risks it. Employers and landlords do not need notice of our past except the relevant details (work history, pay history).

> *Going back to the process, I suggested a therapist first, then transition later. That is the suggested way, even the preferred way. I socially transitioned starting in 1987 but only on a limited basis. Even my 'full time' in 1988 did not including doing so at home in my parent's home. At work and school, I was fully transitioned and 'stealth'. No one knew of my transition. I didn't find a therapist until fall of 1989, two years after starting my transition. And it took them almost three months to decide to accept me into their program (a major university gender clinic).*

By the time the first year is over, we have developed a sense of style and our appearance is congruent with our age and position in society. We have learned to present, our deportment, consistent with our gender. We have begun to have social contacts and, in many cases, work experience. We have stabilized. From here on, we set a goal for SRS.

– REAL LIFE

Whether a transition happens as a teen or adult, it satisfies the need to be our real self, the person we've always known us to be. And as much joy as it brings, the stresses are enormous.

First, the people that know us pretransition have to adjust their own perceptions of who we are, who they always THOUGHT they knew. Most are caught off guard, wondering where this strange concept is coming from. They didn't see anything that suggested we were anything other than what we were born as. Our attempts to hide our nature succeeded well, at least in some ways. Getting used to a new name, and pronouns, and our changing appearances often is too much for some. Others, unable or unwilling to accept our change, or even the concept, reject us out of hand.

Family is often a mixed bag. Much will depend on our parents' attitudes. When we have people that never knew us pre-transition in the same room with those that did, fireworks are possible.

We have work, necessary to provide the funds we need during transition to pay for therapists, doctors, endocrinologists, HRT, lab work and of course wardrobes. Our relationships with those that knew us pretransition and at the start of our transition, evolve or dissolve. And we begin to integrate our two lives. Hell year is followed by our settling into our new normal, our real self. We begin to live as we were meant to all along. It isn't all smooth sailing from here on, on the contrary.

> *Twenty-seven years after I started my transition, twenty-two years after surgery, I met a neighbor at a community function. This 92-year-old, little old woman, took my hand in both of hers and asked, "Are you a trans-sex-u-al, or a les-b-ian?" I told her my partner of 18 years had been a lesbian. She said, "That's wonderful dear!" She patted my hand and moved her motorized wheelchair off to others.*

It is called passing. Or being stealth. When others we meet take us as just another woman or man. They don't hesitate or 'other' us. It takes years for us to relax every time we meet new people. Yet it is fundamental to passing that we be confident in our self. The lack of confidence is noteworthy to people, it catches their attention, and they look closer.

Being clocked, pinged, outed, or just plain confronted is the fear we all face when we start presenting ourselves to the world as WE were meant to be. During the hell year, it happens too often and fear and anxiety which keep us from transitioning sooner, grows. It is the opposite of what we need to happen, but every time we are outed, and it doesn't end in a nightmare of physical altercation, we gain some confidence that we can handle the situation.

Wearing the appropriate clothes, having the correct deportment, being confident all contribute to our ability to blend in and blending in is something we have wanted our entire lives. To meet up with a bunch of girlfriends and have a day of shopping and socializing. To get a gang of guys for a game of soccer or basketball, to hang and have a few beers. To be NORMAL.

Our social life becomes normal. Mostly. There are still things we need to keep to ourselves. We have a body that is not completely correct. Our appearance is only somewhat skin deep. We have medical issues our peers do not have, and we learn there are some things that we need to hide from them. Depending on our sexual orientation, we date with those we always wished we could. But intimacy is still a dangerous place for us.

The last thing we need is for new people in our lives, those that have taken us for our correct gender, to find we were not born into that sex. For us the risk is potentially fatal. People react to us in unexpected ways. That nice guy becomes enraged and violent; that nice girl screams and explodes. And the people around look at us as the cause. If, and it is a rare one, they don't yell about us not being what we appear, people will still look to see what we did to cause the outbursts. Even when it does not become loud and disruptive, the negative responses will provoke greater scrutiny of us.

Fear drives us, from our earliest years through to this day in our transition, and it affects the way we approach tomorrow. But fear is secondary to dysphoria and so we push through. The more we live our life 24/7, the more confidence we have and the better we are at dealing with those confrontations.

The second and third years of transition are spent establishing ourselves and continuing therapy and HRT. As we get more comfortable, the areas we have to continue to hold in secret become a thorn in our lives. We want to be whole, to be able to move fully forward.

– THE MEDICAL AND THERAPIST COMMUNITIES

The medical side of transition is complex and poorly understood outside the transsex community. Many medical professionals want to help and yet, they seldom can grasp the intensity and certainty most of us feel from an early age. They lack the context to fully understand (in the meaning of the UK Court) what dysphoria and the treatment means to us.

We don't want to make the medical transition process so onerous that no one can access care, even minors. But the process MUST be objective enough that those not appropriately suited for a medical transition get the therapy they need but are prevented from access to HRT and surgery.

Despite the last two decades of information, most first points of contact for the gender incongruent in the medical community, are unprepared and uninformed. As the previous section pointed out, treatment of the male and female incongruent, regardless of age, needs to be handled differently. It is not just hormones, but mental health issues also.

What has happened since about the mid-2010s is an acceptance of the idea that a teen or adult can identify as 'trans' and the medical community MUST accept it as complete and accurate. Failure to do so is met with accusations of transphobia. I was told by a licensed therapist that failure to do so, would if reported, result in her license being revoked. This is malpractice; this is an abdication of the responsibility to do no harm to the patient; this is a failure of common sense.

I expected, and continue to do so, the medical community to have treated my dysphoria with skepticism – but not outright rejection, however. We need to get some pushback from the medical community so they can have some confidence they are treating the right conditions. For a patient to specify a diagnosis and treatment plan without the intervention of the medical community's professional skepticism and knowledge is no different than a surgeon operating where and how a patient instructs them.

When the medical community abdicates its responsibilities, we get situations like the case in the UK. But even a cursory examination of YouTube videos of detransitioning teens[35] will net multiple examples of therapist's rubber-stamping patient self-diagnoses and treatment plans. And of patients going around the entire process and starting themselves on hormones unsupervised and often unbeknownst to parents.

WE, those of us that are (were) gender incongruent must bring ourselves to the attention of the medical community. We have to honestly inform them of our situation, our history, and our expectations. But we are also obligated to listen to the professionals in the medical community.

In the past, parents that relied upon therapists (few), were being guided by professionals that were in most cases proponents of the status quo in the mental health professions. Far from helping, their advice often made things considerably worse. These professionals were keepers of societal norms and the incongruent offended their sensibilities far more than that of the parents.

> *If my opinion of mental health professionals seems a little slanted it is because my experience with them, like many of MY peers, was far from helpful. My first gender therapist told me I was a poor candidate for reassignment because I lacked homosexual relationships in my immediate past. In the 70s and early 80s, such relationships could get you beaten or even arrested and by the late 80s, such relationships could expose you to HIV/AIDS. The risk was just too high for me (and my sexual interest mostly non-existent) and for the psychiatrist, it was evidence of a lack of commitment. I of course never went back to him, but he was an example of what was available throughout the 70s, 80s and 90s.*

Therapists today are more likely to jump on any gender non-conformity and lead both the teen and parents into transition talk, even if the teen isn't truly gender incongruent. Other issues are assumed to have their roots in gender incongruency and would therefore be treated by blockers, hormones, and transition. This is dangerous and medically unsound.

---

[35] More about detransitioning

Social difficulties, puberty's medical complications, and familial strains can all be lumped into a gender dysphoria diagnosis that hides other real problems. Unaddressed, those problems will get worse, not better, by transitioning socially and medically. In too many cases over the last 5-7 years, transitioning actually had some positive social benefit even when the medical benefit was dubious at best.

Therapists AND the rest of the medical community have bought into the idea that if a teen or adult claims to be gender incongruent, then they will be treated as such. Objectivity goes out the window. This abdication of responsibility by the medical community is having dire consequences as pointed out by the Bell case in the UK, and the numerous cases of detransitioning young adults.

Those of with gender incongruity must self-identify to parents and the medical community, but it needs to be confirmed over time and with objectivity on the part of the adults. Do not dismiss it but do evaluate it. This has not been happening and parts of the medical community have lost any objectivity. The activist community has pushed the narrative that any identification must be taken as 100% fact and all social and medical transitioning protocols suspended in lieu of full acceptance. This is going to be, and has been, dangerous to many teens.

The push back from those that demand a return to the status quo of denying gender incongruity exists has begun and it is using the treatment (medical and even occasionally surgical) of minors as its root argument. They have a case, which is going to be horrifyingly detrimental to the actual gender incongruent teen (and their parents). Using politics and law to ban treatment for gender dysphoria borders on tyrannical nightmare. Treatment MUST be left between the doctors, their patients, and the parents who MUST be honest and objective about a diagnosis.

The term used by activists and teens is gatekeeper. Someone that puts hoops and bumps in the way of treatment for the gender incongruent. But those hoops are there to help prevent teens, and even adults, from equating their real difficulties, with gender dysphoria when it doesn't really exist, for them.

Most parents turned to either their family physician, who lacked any experience with gender incongruity (if the concept was even known), or to their religious advisor. Remember the previous comments concerning religious discernment? If the family physician lacked experience, and the regional therapist lacked a willingness to consider 'out of the ordinary' situations, the religious advisors often channeled fire and brimstone.

Maybe this seems somewhat an archaic point of view, but even today significant areas in the West and pretty much everywhere else, these ARE the norms.

At the risk of giving a non-incongruent teen (or even adult) the criteria I look for and for which I think is necessary to confirm a diagnosis of gender incongruity by which they can get parents and the medical community to treat them as such, it goes back to the starting premise:

First and foremost, it is the self-knowledge that their body is wrong. NOT that the other sex is RIGHT. The distinction is important, subtle, and very, very easy to mimic. Many non-dysphoric teens will complain about body image, social difficulties of their birth gender, even physical discomfort, and a wish for the simplicity of the other sex's life. They idealize the other sex. They have an idea in their head about how their life would be different if they were the other sex – an echo of how the gender incongruent believes the same. And their nature will have been congruent throughout their pre-puberty years.

Can a teen in puberty realize for the first time they are incongruent? Yes. But I believe it is very rare. Far, far more rare than the current climate suggests. And for an adult to first come to a conclusion of incongruity with no past history and no early nature confusion? Not absolutely impossible, but all but non-existent.

This is why therapy for a period of time is so important with a skilled and objective therapist. Unfortunately, such a therapist is very hard to find.

– ENDOCRINOLOGY AND HORMONES

Once the medical community has been engaged and therapy is involved, a recommendation for hormones is often provided. Hormone replacement therapy (HRT) is a bit of a misnomer for incongruent patients. Often thought of as a treatment for menopause in women and men later in life, HRT is designed to reverse the normal male and female hormone levels in incongruent patients. All men have levels of estrogen, and all women have levels of testosterone. The goal of HRT in the incongruent patient is to attain female levels in the incongruent male and male levels in the incongruent female.

For the young teen, puberty blockers are often the first step IF puberty has not started.

While puberty blockers have been scrutinized by some due to their use in caring for transgender children, these drugs have been in use since the 1980s and are overwhelmingly safe if used appropriately. Side effects such as bone health risks typically only occur with prolonged use past the age of puberty.[36]

Puberty blockers have become a political football and the reason is in some cases, the medical community's quick embrace and use of puberty blockers without clear indication from therapists of their appropriateness. A major organization in the UK[37] was shuttered after whistleblowers pointed out that children were being treated with little or no therapy supporting the use of blockers and HRT. I won't rehash all the points I made previously, but good therapy, strong medical support, and a clear history are necessary prerequisites.

---

[36] Puberty Blockers: https://www.cedars-sinai.org/blog/puberty-blockers-for-precocious-puberty.html

[37] Tavistock was the organization shuttered AND the organization at the heart of the previously discussed court case in Treatment of Minor with Gender Dysphoria section

Endocrinologists are the doctors that usually prescribe hormones. As with medical doctors and therapists, finding one that has some experience and understanding of the needs of incongruent patients is difficult. For those with health care insurance, they are limited as to whom they can go to, and even then, waiting lists can be months, or in the case of some countries, years.

> *I have spent the last 33 years on hormones. I am checked regularly and have had zero complications or issues. But I have also had to spend most of those 33 years educating endocrinologists on appropriate care for my status.*

The first step is to get bloodwork to determine the current hormone levels of both estrogen and testosterone in both incongruent males and females. Occasionally, and this is from anecdotal evidence, the bloodwork shows inappropriate levels before any hormonal changes are made. Males with low testosterone or high estrogen, females with low estrogen or high testosterone happen. If genetic testing is done in this group, as indicated earlier, abnormalities are occasionally found.

Endocrinologists are a conservative bunch. They will start with very low dosages to determine how our bodies handle the change. In my case, and way too many others to be dismissed, our bodies react strongly to the introduction of a cross-sex hormone. It is as if our body is dying of thirst and is given water.

About three months after dosages are started, bloodwork is repeated to determine our body's reaction to the hormone. It is usually at this point an endocrinologist can begin dosages to attain puberty levels. However, on average, the dosage required to reach those appropriate levels are significantly higher than endocrinologist's have historically been comfortable with.

Often, the endocrinologist will treat is if our current biological age is the determinant for dosage levels. This is wrong. The introduction of a cross-sex hormone will introduce a second puberty to the incongruent patient. And the appropriate level is puberty levels of hormones. This level must be maintained throughout the average puberty period, five to seven years.

High doses of hormones can cause problems for congruent adults and endos are very reluctant, often refuse, to prescribe appropriate dosages. The problem, generally with the incongruent male, with standard dosages is they are often insufficient to actually promote the second puberty necessary to begin physical transition.

For the incongruent female, testosterone is a powerful hormone that will often dramatically change his body very quickly. Hair growth, fat distribution, voice change, and muscle growth can begin as quickly as six weeks after beginning HRT.

Endocrinologists want us to understand the changes and how fast, or slow, they may come. They will tell us about the risks (to anyone taking a hormone) and the possible side effects. Of course, to us, the side effects are what we are looking for: changes in our bodies. But having a realistic view of what can be accomplished is important. An incongruent female, age 18, that is 5'1", will likely remain 5'1" regardless of the hormone dose. An incongruent male, age 18, that is 6'2" will not shrink on HRT!

It should be noted that teens presenting themselves to places for hormones without therapy (or sometimes even parental awareness) are likely to have incorrect impressions about what hormones can and can't do. Endocrinologists that prescribe hormones in such cases are medically, ethically and in my opinion, legally, engaged in malpractice. Reliance upon a letter from a therapist who only saw the patient once does not change that situation. Even if the patient is an adult in these circumstances doesn't change that situation.

Many of the changes brought by HRT are very welcome. However, there is one that we understand intellectually that will have an emotional impact that politicians and others than the incongruent focus strongly on: infertility. We know we are giving up the possibility of children. We've known since we learned of the ability to physical transition that there will be no biological children for us in the future.

For those that already have children prior to transition, this is less of a concern. For those that are transitioning in the teen years, adults will argue they can't understand the emotional consequence of infertility (a factor in the UK case). They are quite wrong. We know what we are giving up. Willingly. What most people do not realize is that the use of our natal sex gonads is, offensive. The idea of procreative sex, heck, any sexual interaction, in our natal sex, makes us emotionally, and often physically, sick.

The incongruent male would love to have children. To conceive, to carry a baby to term, to give birth and to breastfeed is an emotional holy grail. But to have penetrative sex? Gawd no. I won't say we don't try. I did. But our emotional state makes the effort more or less fruitless and infrequent at best. The incongruent female would love to have children also, but to carry a baby? He already hates menses and the changes a pregnancy would make in his body makes it all but impossible to consider[38]. And to let someone penetrate? OH HELL NO.

HRT in the incongruent male takes months before even the smallest changes begin. It can take a year before there is any significant change. And if stopped in that time, most of the changes fade quickly. For the incongruent female, the changes happen quickly and do not fade or even reverse if HRT is stopped. This is one of the major reasons why the medical community (and therapists) need to treat the incongruent female differently than the incongruent male. We are different. We react differently to HRT. The consequences are different.

Some people mistake a change in the body from hormones to suggest aspects of puberty are reversed. They are not. A male that goes through puberty has systemic and foundational changes that even years on estrogen will not reverse or change. Skeleton structure and many organ developments will remain for their life – the same type of changes the female will have after puberty. While some musculature change does occur, it does not change to 'norms' associated with natal structures.

> *I played on the golf team in high school and continued to play well into my 50s. During and after my transition, I was asked to play with women in amateur competitions. I refused because it was clear, even 10 years on HRT, that I had an unfair advantage over other women.*
>
> *Prior to puberty, I see no issue with boys and girls competing against each other. Once puberty has*

---

[38] There have been some (few) that have become pregnant so that they could have a biological child yet expect to fully transition. Having a biological child also prevents, usually, courts from removing the child in the future over the parent's transition.

begun, that is problematic and after puberty, I think it should be prohibited. Just because testosterone levels are reduced or very low, doesn't mean all the other structural changes no longer exist.

So far, we have talked about the physical changes. HRT has a psychological and emotional impact also. Almost all of us notice a change mentally within the first couple of weeks on HRT. Our brains begin to work better. Emotionally we are happier. Not just because we began HRT, but because the impact on our brain is much quicker than on our body. I argue, as do many others, that because our brain had been sensitized to the hormone differently than our biological sex, the introduction of the correct hormone has an almost immediate positive impact.

My emotional changes made my desire for emotional control much more difficult. I had learned to protect myself over the years from expressing emotions inconsistent with my natal sex. Because I socially transitioned two and half years before getting HRT, I had an established feminine personality and HRT made that difficult to emotionally maintain. An example: crying in public. Something I hadn't done since about 8 or 9 because it got be beaten worse by the bullies. After HRT, context appropriately, crying in public was almost impossible to stop from happening.

I consider it an element of confirmation of appropriate treatment when the mental state of the incongruent patient improves on HRT. It is a red flag to ME, if the mental state does not improve.

If the mental state of the patient gets worse on HRT, it is a clear sign that 1) HRT needs to be stopped until their mental health improves, 2) that other issues are in play that suggest gender incongruity is not the root mental health issue.

The physical changes brought on by HRT help us during transition. It helps our body reflect our true sex. For the incongruent female, he grows facial hair, body hair, his voice drops, and musculature begins to form. The body fat distribution caused by puberty begins to decrease and redistribute. What breast development that occurred decreases, somewhat. It will not remove breast tissue, which will need surgery. For the incongruent male, the fat distribution changes, increases on hips and breasts. Breast development occurs and becomes noticeable. Of course, her voice will not change without effort, but many find a comfortable voice without surgery.

For both, changes in body means changes in wardrobes. But HRT and the necessary bloodwork to maintain appropriate levels costs money even if health insurance covers much. Combined with regular doctor and therapist visits, we face financial costs many never see in their life.

Normal puberty can take five to seven years. Our second puberty can last as long and yet, we are often well past our teen years when we begin HRT. The emotional and physical changes that people accepted and allowed for amongst teens are frowned upon during the adult years. If HRT and social transition occur at the same time, HRT is addition to the hell that the first year brings.

Many teens now are demanding HRT in order to avoid the problems puberty creates for us in adulthood. I sympathize. However, without support of family, without good therapy, without some time to understand and accept the future, HRT will complicate rather than help the situation. I still support minors getting blockers, and after a couple of years on therapy and blockers, HRT. But, right now, I have zero confidence in the medical community (therapists, endocrinologists, and surgeons) to act ethically. And parents are being railroaded into accepting 'affirmative care'.

HRT is a life-long requirement once started. It is an acceptable cost for the benefits, and consequences, it brings.

– SURGERY : SEX REASSIGNMENT SURGERY

For decades, the primary surgery for incongruent patients has been called sex reassignment surgery or SRS. In recent years it has been called gender confirmation surgery or GCS. Regardless of what it is called in the media, or the medical community, we call it bottom surgery. Whatever the name, it doesn't change the nature of the procedures. This surgery will change the genital area to appear consistent with our gender. For the incongruent male, this surgery has been well developed and can be very natural looking and functional. For the incongruent female, improvements have been happening but at a slower, and more costly rate. Appearances have improved but recreating a fully functional penis is still beyond our medical capabilities at this point.

For the incongruent female, there are two intermediate steps prior to SRS: breast and reproductive organ removal. The former is often done early in transition. The latter can often be done at the same time as the first step in SRS.

After several years of transition, HRT, and therapy, we begin, well, we start getting more ready for SRS. In the last five years the cost for sex reassignment surgery for the incongruent male, called vaginoplasty, has more than doubled primarily because demand has gone through the roof. Also, insurance will now cover the surgery (in some cases via private employers, in others via State willingness to cover via Medicaid). For the incongruent female, there are three surgeries: top surgery or mastectomy; hysterectomy; and then bottom surgery or phalloplasty/metoidioplasty. While the cost of the first two are manageable because many congruent women need the same surgeries, the bottom surgery cost is almost out of reach for anyone without insurance covering all or part.

This is a final step, and it needs our therapists to agree we are ready. Therapists, plural. One of the unchanging requirements over the last 50 years has been approval from two therapists that have known and treated the patient for at least one year. Most of us spend more than a year. Unfortunately, in the last couple of years, therapists have all but been rubberstamping approval without significant understanding if the surgery is appropriate for their patients.

However, it happens, there are choices for where the surgery is performed. In the US and UK, the costs are prohibitive unless insurance is involved. Surgeons in Canada and Asia can be considerably less expensive. Interestingly, Asia (specifically Thailand) has a bad reputation for surgical outcomes yet the state-of-the-art surgery for the incongruent male, at this point, was developed and perfected there.

My surgery was performed in Canada in 1993. There are great surgeons, good surgeons, and those people need to avoid. Every surgeon has a bad outcome on occasion. But the more frequently they perform the surgery, the less likely they will have one on any one particular patient. Still, surgery is major and carries risks. Risks we accept. And issues are common, but usually minor. Waiting lists for the top surgeons can be years, but on average, it is eight to twelve months.

Many people are very scared of bottom surgery. Online communities are rife with misinformation and scary stories of botched surgeries. It is difficult to separate the truth from all the noise. There is pain. It is major surgery. But it is short-lived and manageable. And like HRT, there are maintenance requirements.

NOTE: FOR THE SQUEMISH, THE FOLLOWING DISCUSSES THE AFTERMATH OF SURGERY

For vaginoplasty, the nerve clusters of the head of the penis are used for the clitoris and the surgical trauma shuts down the nerve impulses for 24-36 hours. Pain medication post-surgery manages normal levels, however, when those nerves begin to reawaken, the pain medication is far from sufficient. Everyone tends to know this happens, but it doesn't change the process. It can take 18 to 24 hours to get this increased pain under control.

Several days later, packing that had been used to maintain the vaginal canal open is removed and shortly thereafter, a process called dilation is started. Dilation is using hard plastic dilators into the vaginal cavity several times a day for months, tapering over time but using increasingly thicker dilators. Dilation is also a lifelong chore unless intercourse is engaged in regularly. A common refrain: you have to keep the wound open forever. Well, it isn't really a wound in the sense of a tear in the skin. Akin to getting a piercing, if left unused for a long enough period, the vagina will close. For vaginoplasty that uses inversion (the most common), the exterior of the penis becomes the interior of the vagina, so by one perspective, there is no wound.

For incongruent females there are two different procedures: metoidioplasty or phalloplasty. For metoidioplasty, the clitoris has been enlarged via HRT and tissue is harvested from his body to increase size and provide shaping. Phalloplasty generally results in a larger penis, but the procedure takes multiple surgeries over an extended period of time. Like vaginoplasty, there is pain.

Scaring is minimal for vaginoplasty if done well. And while there is some scaring for the phalloplasty, it is usually at the site the tissue is harvested from.

*

Many are concerned about the pain, appearance, and function after surgery. In most cases, the pain is manageable, appearance is well within norms for natal women, and for the majority intercourse is normal and sensitivity results in organism. These ARE concerns that we need to be aware of and consider. There can also be complications, though in most cases they are minor. But bad surgeries happen. In every kind of surgery. It does not negate the value, nor should it cause the surgery to be removed from access.

Recovery from the surgery takes time. Today, surgeons recommend months of recovery time. In the past, two or three weeks was all we could afford away from work or others without explanation. However long a patient takes, recovery takes time. Most people take six months to reach some semblance of normality.

The pain, the recovery, the chores, don't matter. We are whole. As best as the surgeons could do at the time. We are ready to move on.

Post-surgery the pain meds I was given didn't work. Nor did the next type, or the type after that. Finally, on the night of the second day, I got some relief. The next morning, my packing was removed, and they let me take a shower. A clean nightgown, clean bedding, and clean me allowed me for the first time to really embrace what I had done and notice, no more dysphoria. I started crying. A nurse came in and was concerned the pain had returned.

No, for the first time in my life, I was crying with joy.

The media portrayal of SRS, at least those that reject the concept of gender incongruity or the process of treating it, ignores the years of effort and travails we endure and some of the medical literature.[39]. It seems they think we wake up, decide to change our sex, and a few months later we get surgery and pretend something has changed.

"Nothing you do can change a man into a woman!"

What do you mean by 'man' or 'woman'? If you are talking about chromosomal male/female, you are correct. If you are talking about physical sex, our secondary sexual characteristics, you are incorrect. And finally, if you are talking about the emotional, psychological, and expression that separates a man from a woman in the view of others, you are most certainly wrong.

"You are deluded, and I'm not going to join you in your delusion."

We are rejected. So be it. We have fought to get to where we are, and we are finally free to live our lives. People think they can always tell if a person was transsex or not. Most do not realize they have walked right past us without any recognition on their part. I know a couple of natal women

---

[39] As noted earlier, there is a lot of medical literature that contradicts itself in this area. Cherry picking goes on from both sides of the arguments over medical transition.

who have been accused of being transsex. Most of us are unnoticed because that is what we want.

And now, with surgery done, the fear of intimacy and being 'caught' with the wrong genitals, is gone. Our gender dysphoria is gone. We can relax, put the constant anxiety aside.

– POST TRANSITION

For the majority of us, SRS signals the end of our transition. We have reached the other side of our travels. Going forward, we will maintain our new genitals and hormones, but there is nothing left to reach for. Except the life we hoped for. Relationships, careers, families.

For a significant portion, there is still some therapy to be done. The issues caused by our childhood, puberty and later still need some resolutions. But for everyone I have ever talked to, over a hundred that have had surgery, gender dysphoria is gone. Evaporated. It is like a pain you had learned to live with, that had always been present, was suddenly no longer there.

There are things we will have to deal with for the rest of our lives. There will be medical issues where the medical community will need to know about our past. But most such times will be few. People that knew us long ago and exited our lives back then will pop up and not know about our transition. I have several people that I knew in high school that are friends now. And family.

Some that rejected us early in our transitions, or even before, decide to return. If the damage is not great, and they fully accept us now, we usually welcome them back into our lives. But others remain antagonistic.

Hopefully, we don't pretend our past didn't happen, but we have moved on and try not to dwell there. I say hopefully because many people, not just us, live in the past. Rehashing events over and over again hoping to see something different than what actually happened.

So, the question for us after surgery is, what's next? For all of our lives we had this goal, which seemed almost impossible in the beginning and felt impossible so often during our travel towards it. Now, many are adrift, not sure what to do.

Two items will cause us the most concern during our future: intimate relationships and children. What do we tell intimate partners, or when? The appropriate time is before the relationship reaches that point, at least if you listen to the majority. However, probably for the better, such relationships often die on the vine of that disclosure. It becomes hard to withhold the information, but also to risk the relationship.

For the incongruent male, she is likely indistinguishable from a natal woman. She of course cannot bear children so that is an issue that must be addressed. Most of us have had sexual partners and even doctors that were unaware of our history. But the desire to be honest usually wins and the relationship continues, or more often, ends.

For the incongruent female, he has a much more difficult time presenting in intimate situations and most are up front early in any dating situation.

For both, children are usually hoped for. Obviously, adoption is the most common avenue but potential partners that already have children can often soften any risk that being unable to bear or father children might cause a growing relationship.

It may not be necessary to ever tell children about a parent's biological nature, but I think most of us do. I did. In the West, today, younger adults have fewer issues with transsex. Still, when is a concern. Waiting until they are adults can, has, backfired. And teens are not great secret keepers.

Once in a relationship, our partners often have to consider how much, if anything, to tell their family and friends. The complications our history causes do not end with transition.

There is one other set of relationships that offer some complications. It is not uncommon for friendships to end if our past is revealed. So, we learn to withhold much of our past from new friends and certainly from casual acquaintances. But some friendships last years and we talk about our past, changing names and pronouns where appropriate but, generally, we keep the history otherwise true. To do otherwise just complicates things.

Both those friendships, like any relationship, are based on trust and when those friends find out about our past, they feel we have lied to them. That any foundation of the friendship had been based on lies. It is hard to dispute their position – most of us don't try except to ask, when was a good time to say something?

There is no easy answer because we learn that people, regardless of how liberal and accepting they may be in general, tend to be very different when confronted with our gender incongruity directly. Not everyone, but...

Most demand we should have said something right at the beginning. Again, it would be hard to dispute it IF we knew the casual meeting would turn into a friendship. And by the time it has, any delay would be just as damning.

Until very recently, exposure of our past has been very damaging to relationships, to workplaces, to community involvement. People reject us. Employers terminate with little fear of consequences. And organizations demand our exit. In recent years, but mostly amongst younger generations, there is acceptance. So, many it will be less of an issue in the future.

➢ *Detransitioning*

Detransitioners are people that have gone through transition, often with a full period (years) of hormone treatment, and surgeries and yet found themselves no better, and often worse off. Their plight, when brought to a skeptical public reinforces the idea that transitioning is wrong, or bad. But listening to or reading their stories you find several consistent, or at least oft repeated components:

1. Undiagnosed or unresolved childhood trauma. Probably the most common element is some aspect of abuse in early childhood. To be honest, we are not honest about the bad things that happen to us, and when children are abused, they learn not to trust any adults. Sexual abuse is the most common of those abuses and it happens to both male and female, but girls take the biggest brunt of it. Is it any wonder when they reject their femininity in every form? And young males, assaulted by other males, often want nothing to do with their sex. Both look to the other sex believing that if they had been the other sex, the assault never would have happened. Possibly. But their reaction and rejection need the context to be understood before gender dysphoria is diagnosed.

2. Gender non-conforming being immediately diagnosed as gender dysphoria. Kids learn many things as they grow but if given freedom, they will experiment across a broad range of behaviors that adults might consider incongruent or non-conforming behaviors. It doesn't mean either are applicable but nervous parents, or professionals with their own ideas can equate those behaviors with incongruity and provide a diagnosis that fixes many children on a specific path. It is true that many gender non-conforming grow out of their behaviors as they get older and might be prevented by an incorrect gender dysphoria diagnosis.

3. Ill equipped or poorly trained therapists. The subtle differences between non-conforming, dysmorphia and dysphoria are difficult for any parent to distinguish. When therapists have had few or no experiences with children (or even adults) presenting any of the above, they often will claim a diagnosis that might be, often is, wrong.

4. Few or little therapist interactions. No reputable surgeon will perform SRS on a teen (generally not allowed at this point) or adult without letters from therapists noting the diagnosis and period of treatment. Yet,

therapists are providing such letters with often as few as ONE therapy session. And surgeons are accepting such letters when there is clear evidence that such affirmation is inconsistent. There is little chance that any therapist is going to get a full and complete history AND be able to know the veracity of it AND be able to come to a serious conclusion of gender dysphoria in one, or even several sessions.

5. Surgeons, and gender clinics, that support, approve or perform surgery on minors are WRONG. The political fallout for those medical professionals that refuse to treat (provide hormones or surgery) is substantial. Therapists are told they will lose their license if a 'trans kid' is denied hormones or surgery based on their assessment. Political pressure is applied to prevent ANY argument against 'affirmative care'. Children are presenting consistent with their biological sex, but demanding cross-sex hormones. The political climate is destroying kids.

Detransitioners are often the result of a failure of the system to adequately treat patients individually. There is no single correct way to deal with each of us, and many wrong ways to do so. I want as few Detransitioners to go through the hell it must be to get to a place of healthy and happy.

The way we do that is with knowledgeable therapists and a medical community objectively treating patients. But if the medical community will not police itself, if it will not abide by consistent medical ethical rules, then banning the care may be the only option. Note that doing so will harm those that are actually gender incongruent.

WPATH, World Professional Association for Transgender Health, has abandoned the transsex community it was originally founded to help. It has done so to support a political position, affirmative care for transgender (note, not transsex) patients. I do not consider its ethical guidelines to be sufficient, or even beneficial, to any patient seeking gender oriented care.

A FINAL WORD

What do most of us want? To be normal. Just like everyone else. We can't have that, so we do what we can. Most, after SRS, fade into the woodwork of normal society. Try to live our lives as if the horrors of gender incongruity never happened.

For myself and almost all of us, alleviating the dysphoria, having normal interactions with people, and finding some measure of happiness was worth the effort.

APPENDIX

– WHEN DOES GENDER APPEAR

Your baby's gender is determined at the moment of conception — when the sperm contributed a Y chromosome, which creates a boy, or an X chromosome, which creates a girl. Boys' and girls' genitals develop along the same path with no outward sign of gender until about nine weeks.[40]

Of course, what they are discussing is the baby's biological SEX. To get to gender, we need a different focus.

Most children between ages 18 and 24 months can recognize and label gender groups. They may identify others as girls, women or feminine. Or they may label others as boys, men, or masculine. Most also label their own gender by the time they reach age 3.

However, society tends to have a narrow view of gender. As a result, some children learn to behave in ways that may not reflect their gender identity. At age 5 or 6, most children are rigid about gender and preferences.[41]

Also:

2 to 3 years old:

- At around 2 years old, children are aware of differences between boys and girls.

- Most children can identify themselves as a "boy" or "girl". This term may or may not match the assigned sex at birth.

- Some children's gender identity remains stable over their life, while others may alternate between

---

[40] UT Southwestern Medical Center: https://utswmed.org/medblog/gender-prediction/
[41] Mayo Clinic: https://www.mayoclinic.org/healthy-lifestyle/childrens-health/in-depth/children-and-gender-identity/art-20266811

identifying themselves as "boy" or "girl", or even assume other gender identities at different times (sometimes even in the same day). This is normal and healthy.

4 to 5 years old:

- While many children at this age have a stable gender identity, gender identity may change later in life.

- Children become more aware of gender expectations or stereotypes as they grow older. For example, they may think that certain toys are only for girls or boys.

- Some children may express their gender very strongly. For example, a child might go through a stage of insisting on wearing a dress every day or refusing to wear a dress even on special occasions.

6 to 7 years old:

- Many children begin to reduce outward expressions of gender as they feel more confident that others recognize their gender. For example, a girl may not feel that she has to wear a dress every day because she knows that others see her as a girl no matter what she wears.

- Children who feel their gender identity is different from the assigned sex at birth may experience increased social anxiety because they want to be like their peers, but realize they don't feel the same way.[42]

And:

Kohlberg suggested that by the age of 2 or 2 1/2 years children acquire a basic understanding of gender and label themselves as girls or boys. After the age of 3 years, children have an understanding that boys become men and girls become women. Between the ages of 5 and 7 years, Kohlberg

---

[42] https://caringforkids.cps.ca/handouts/behavior-and-development/gender-identity

Obviously, there is no clear consistency in the literature. My observation, opinion, is based on conversations amongst us about when we started to be aware. Although there are those that knew earlier, the four to seven years old assertion seems broadly consistent with research.

---

[43] Counseling Women Across the Life Span: Empowerment, Advocacy, and Intervention. By Jill Schwarz, PhD, NCC

– HOW MANY TRANSSEX PEOPLE ARE THERE?

From the numbers used in Introduction, the proffered study finding the number of transsex to be 4.6/100,000, we have a community size of about 15,180 in the United States and 368,000 worldwide.

According to DSM-5-TR, the prevalence of gender dysphoria is 0.005–0.014% for adult natal males and 0.002-0.003% for adult natal females[44] resulting in a total population of about 56,000 in the US and 1,360,000 worldwide.

From the Vrije Universiteit Amsterdam study quoted in the Introduction, using the prevalence of 1 of 2,800 and 1 of 5,200 for males and females, gives us a US community size of around 90,000 and 2,169,000 worldwide.

I think the above vastly underestimates the community size[45]. There are other reported numbers. From *Demographic and temporal trends in transgender identities and gender confirming surgery*[46]

Parameter * estimated percent of total US population. TGNB, transgender and gender non-binary; GCS, gender confirming surgery	**Range of estimated prevalence among transgender people in the USA, % (Ref.)**
TGNB identity*	0.39–2.7* (1,3-6)
GCS overall	25–35 (7,8)

TGNB is the number of people identifying as transgender, .39 to 2.7%. This indicates a population in the United States at between 1,287,000 and 8,910,000.

---

[44] Carolina Center for Behavioral Health: https://emedicine.medscape.com/article/2200534-overview
[45] Studies require volunteers or self-identified individuals. Something we have learned to limit as much as possible. Large surveys allow for more anonymity.
[46] New York School of Medicine: https://www.ncbi.nlm.nih.gov/pmc/articles/PMC6626314/

Because transsex generally plan on surgery and transgender does not, the surgical number might be more representative of the transsex community size. Note that in the literature it is generally accepted that top surgery and hysterectomy surgery are considered in the Gender Confirmation Surgery totals. I only consider bottom surgery as SRS/GCS. Still, 25% of the above range would be 321,750-2,228,000.

My own argument is that for each one of us that has SRS, that there are two in transition, and for each one in transition, there are two that seek to do so. Using the surgical number, it puts the community size between 2,252,00 and 8,900,000. Pretty close to the Demographic study.

The estimates I provided were .25% to .40%, putting the US population between 825,000 and 1,320,000. Slightly smaller but probably closer to the historical averages. Worldwide our community would be 20 to 32 million.

I think the upper number is less likely to be correct based on other's findings, but even my experience is limited to the US and UK. What the prevalence is in Asia or Africa is unknown. We assume that what we know in the US/UK is similar to those continents, but we cannot know sufficiently in my opinion to guess. The upper number considers current prevalence and estimates reported in studies.

Whatever the size of the community, based on the number of people on the planet, we are a small subset. The transgender community's outsized influence politically over the last ten years, beneficial in getting our community recognized and to some extent accepted, has become harmful.

- DES

For a subset of us, those born in the 50s and 60s mostly, there is still the question of why, but HOW might have a possible answer.

There is a strong possibility that my mother received DES during her pregnancy with me. It was a drug used in the late 50s and early 60s to help women that had a previous miscarriage as did my mother.

Diethylstilbestrol (DES) is a synthetic form of the female hormone estrogen. It was prescribed to pregnant women between 1940 and 1971 to prevent miscarriage, premature labor, and related complications of pregnancy (1). The use of DES declined after studies in the 1950s showed that it was not effective in preventing these problems, although it continued to be used to stop lactation, for emergency contraception, and to treat menopausal symptoms in women (2).[47]

There is a LOT of discussion, in the community and amongst some of the medical community about a link between DES and gender incongruity development in the children exposed to invitro. Some claims, as high as 40% of boys born to women that had taken DES during the pregnancy cannot be verified, primarily because there have been no valid studies. And given the ages of the mothers at this point (and the number that have died), there is never likely to be any.

Still, the evidence that DES affects male development IS pretty conclusive in animal studies. Could the general explosion of incongruent males (and to a degree females) born in the 50s and 60s be related to the drug? And if so, how do you explain the much larger surge after 2000?

I, like most others, did not know of DES until recently. In my case after my mother had died. The medical community does not like finding out

---

[47] Cancer.gov: https://www.cancer.gov/about-cancer/causes-prevention/risk/hormones/des-fact-sheet

something they supported had unintended negative consequences. Whatever the truth, it is something that will be tantalizing, but fundamentally, unverifiable, and unsatisfying.

144

- IT'S POLITICS

I have tried (and failed, mostly) to stay away from the political arguments, even some of the social ones. My reasoning being - most of the activist's efforts "on behalf of the trans" community are so detrimental to the actual transsex person that, generally, as a group, we oppose much of it. So much so that many transsex people reject 'trans' and want nothing to do with activist efforts. Many of us are OK with removing trans health care from minors **ONLY BECAUSE** the current climate does not adequately vet or protect those for whom HRT and surgery are wrong. We want minors to get medical care - we remember the damage puberty caused to all, repeat ALL, of us. But we don't trust the medical community and therapists right now because they are compromised by a 'trans agenda' such that any who try to actively vet are threatened professionally. Any argument, and Abigail Sherer's attempt is an example of pointing out a real problem, gets hammered from within the trans community, the trans "allies" and the media.

We are a small part of the trans community, which itself is probably only 1% of the larger community (but 3-4% of the current Gen Z). And any contra-voices that do get out, are mob tackled and removed as quickly as possible. The political heft of the trans community is magnified by the LGBT (though not so much the Lesbians), the politicians - both sides - and the media.

All of the above is part of the arguments being made by 'supported authors' on both sides. Both are cherry picking studies and arguments to support their POV. Getting into that mess just adds to the confusion. I just want to offer our experience.

I want people to understand us first, then reach whatever POV works for them.

- WHAT IS A WOMAN?

What is a Woman is a recent documentary where the title
question is asked, and the responses discussed. For the Host and many
supporters, the correct response is, a mature human female. Hard to
dispute that but of course he found many, many, who would and did do so.
He is not inaccurate, as far as the discussion goes, but he is reducing
women to a fixed biological state, rather than the complex human we all
are as our adult selves. We are more than just our biology. We are not
bound by nature's instincts – for better or worse. We can exceed those
strict biological limits. Men and women are mature humans, but they are
also complex individuals.

"OH, I'M MALE,' HE SAID WITH A LAUGH. "BUT NOT NECESSARILY A MAN.
THAT'S A STATE OF MIND RATHER THAN A QUESTION OF BIOLOGY."

"MAIN STREET DRAG" BY MARYANNE PETERS 2021

As is being a woman. There are many 50-year-old males that have
no understanding of what it is to be a man. And many 40-year-old females
living forever in their teen years. Maturity is not just about age, or biology,
but about understanding adulthood.

Of course, where does that put the transwoman? In the Host's
estimation, a delusional male. Certainly nothing like a mature human
female. But how would you tell a transwoman from a natal woman? For
most of us, a much higher percentage than the Host would imagine, you
would need a blood test to know our biological origin – and if we are
indistinguishable from natal women in our day to day lives, what difference
does it make to the general public? Unless we start carrying around
evidence of our genetic foundations, duly presented upon demand, what is
the expectation?

Of all the characteristics that can be used to describe a woman, her
SEX, obvious to all (?), is probably pretty far down the list. Every one of

those characteristics is shared by 'trans women.' To dismiss them is to reduce all women.

Many of the same arguments are of course appropriate to transmen also. A question I often ask in discussions about the documentary, would you want a trans man, sharing a bathroom with a wife or daughter? Looking at photos of transmen, most men would reject that idea out of hand.

ACKNOWLEDGMENT

Asking someone to review, to comment and make suggestions on a book that deals with controversial topics is difficult. Several agreed but asked me not to use their name here. Their comments and suggestions helped immensely.

One that was fine with including his name, I am limiting myself to just his first name: Hanno. His insightful questions and suggestions help make this a better book. I can't thank him enough.

One other was particularly helpful with editing and clarifying (read fixing my grammar). I even included a quote from her. Thanks to my little mermaid.

I alone am responsible for any remaining errors.